Broken by Beauty

'Purity is mocked, trampled, and far too often stolen in today's world. Joy's honest and vulnerable journey to hold onto purity is a wake-up call for those who have given up on its relevance. For the broken and grieving, Joy's story is a message of hope. This is a much needed message in the church and beyond.'

Annie Dieselberg – Founder and CEO, NightLight International

'This book, in which Joy is transparently honest, will speak to anyone who wants to make a difference in God's world. As you read Joy's story, you can't help but be captivated by her passion and by the way God has prepared her and fuelled her to fulfil his call on her life. I wholeheartedly recommend you read it, but expect to be challenged – it's not for the faint hearted.'

Nic and Jenny Harding – Senior Pastors of Frontline Church, Liverpool; Author of *Manifesto: A Blueprint for Missional Church*

'"I want my legacy to be purity. I don't want to fall prey to the cheap replicas of love and intimacy . . ." Stated at the age of 15, Joy Farrington's goal has seen God lead her through many sexually impure environments: bringing healing to her own heart and then breaking it for those desperately snared in the sex industry and the many, many lost in lust and false intimacy. Through experiences living in a red-light district; getting into wrong relationships and having to face the brokenness and need of her own heart; dealing with shame; befriending prostitutes; and encountering the deeply broken lives at the heart of Thailand's sex trade – Joy's beautifully honest account uncovers with candour, openness, transparency and the power of unashamed truth how one young girl is facing the battles and wrestles of her own inner needs to find a call to *love*; and how you can too.'

Jonathan & Heather Bellamy – Cross Rhythms Leadership

'This is a book full of truth, honesty, adventure and hope, even when the world seems hopeless. It has brought me to tears, made me smile and guided me further towards God's heart for me and his creation through Joy's heart-breaking honesty as she shares the highs and lows of her journey so far. I have had the utter privilege of having Joy in my life since we met as enthusiastic and naive 18 year olds, and she remains one of my wisest friends, bringing true love and joy from whichever part of the world she is currently frequenting! We have travelled our own journeys (crossing paths less than I wish we could) as we have sought to bring Christ-like justice to those who are being sexually exploited around us, and I believe this is a valuable book for all to read and reflect on, from a teenage girl struggling to answer the question of "who am I?" to the person who believes their past experiences have made them "tainted goods" for Christian purity. *Broken by Beauty* reveals the true heart of God for each of his children, whether in Bangkok or Birmingham. Joy doesn't sit in judgement and preach from afar, but gets alongside you in the dust, and points you to the Father who brings true freedom. I love her, and you will too!!'

Beth Stout – Director of Golddigger Trust

'*Broken by Beauty* is a beautifully written, honest journey through Joy's heart as she unravels topics of sexual exploitation, human trafficking and sexual purity all through the lens of her own experiences. Joy is a woman who cares deeply about the state of people's hearts and this is clearly shown in the vulnerability of her writing. We have known Joy for nearly fifteen years, watching her grow and mature from a young girl into a woman whose passion for people's freedom is kindred to our own.'

Chris & Kerry Cole – Founders of Cross Rhythms

'*Broken by Beauty* by Joy Farrington is so vulnerably done and it takes you through her own experience as if you were sitting on the shoulder of her consciousness listening to her inner monologue. It's very easy to relate to and is a story of overcoming, a story of walking out an extraordinary perspective but from a woman who could be anyone . . . your sister, your wife, your best friend, even your daughter. The sexual purity and human trafficking content hits the right purity vein and will inspire you to see some things about the world, yourself, and especially being touched by the love of God.'

Shawn Bolz – Personality; Speaker; Senior Pastor of Expression58 Christian Church, Los Angeles; Author of *Keys to Heaven's Economy*, *The Throne Room Company*, *Nonreligious Guide to Dating*

'It (this book – the heart of it) is going to be a beacon shining in dark places, not only for the unsaved but also the church. It's a message that really needs to be proclaimed in these times.

Sarah Simpson – Sales Representative, Cornerstone Vision

'There is nothing that brings me more joy than stories like this; seeing a daughter of God, set free and released into the fullness he created her for. Joy's story (so far) is proof of God's powerful act of restoration and turnaround in people's lives. Knowing Joy as I do and reading the words in this book convince me even more that what the enemy intends for evil, God turns for good, that 'he always wins'. This book is real, beautifully written with powerful insights of a love that is courageous, fearless and does conquer all. You will read this and be so encouraged and challenged that, as we bring brokenness to God, he will make something beautiful out of it.'

Tamsin Evans – Founder & Director of Pure Creative Arts

Broken by Beauty

A Journey from Purity to Restoration & Hope

Joy Farrington

Authentic

Copyright © 2013 Joy Farrington

19 18 17 16   7 6 5 4 3 2

First published 2013 by Authentic Media Limited
PO Box 6326, Bletchley, Milton Keynes, MK1 9GG.
www.authenticmedia.co.uk

The right of Joy Farrington to be identified as the author of this work
has been asserted by her in accordance with the Copyright,
Designs andPatents Act 1988.

British Library Cataloguing in Publication Data

A catalogue record for this book is available from the British Library

ISBN 978-1-78078-057-3
978-1-78078-325-3 (e-book)

The names of some individuals have been changed to protect their identities.

Scripture quotations taken from The Holy Bible, New International
Version (Anglicised edition). Copyright ©1979, 1984, 2011 by Biblica
(formerly International Bible Society). Used by permission of Hodder &
Stoughton Publishers, an Hachette UK company. All rights
reserved. 'NIV' is a registered trademark of Biblica (formerly
International Bible Society). UK trademark number 1448790.

Cover Design by David McNeill (www.reocreative,co,uk)
Printed and bound by CPI Group (UK) Ltd., Croydon, CR0 4YY

Acknowledgements

This book with all of its stories, laughs and tears has only come about because of the wonderful people that fill my life and my awesome Father in heaven who has continued to bless me by the doors that he has opened and the keys that he has entrusted me with. I am constantly overwhelmed by how much he has done for me and the immense power of his love and grace.

I would not have been able to do half the things that I have done so far in my life if it wasn't for my parents who have loved me unconditionally, released me and believed in every dream that I have dared to utter. My siblings continue to inspire and encourage me with their love and their own crazy adventures. Thank you, family, for such a great inheritance and for not giving up on me even when I wanted you to; I am so in love with you all!

The entrance of one character in this book has completely rocked my world ever since and I am so excited for the adventures that are still to be had with them in the years to come. Phillip Attmore, thank you for loving me, fighting for me, pursuing me and being more than I could ever wish for in a partner for life. I know the dreams are only going to get bigger from here!

It stuns me to think of the people in my life who have dared to believe in me, see the gold when all I was holding was dust and whose words and actions have spurred me on to continue fighting and be all that I was created to be. Nick and Tamsin, Nic and Jenny, Chris and Kerry and Jonathan and Heather, I want to thank you from the bottom of my heart for every sacrifice you have made, every wise word spoken and every prayer uttered on my behalf. The impact you have had on my life can only be described as eternal.

There is a whole list of people who come to mind whose friendship, love and support is so dear to my heart and who I absolutely adore! In particular I want to thank the incomparable brother and sister team Natalie and Graham Haywood for their constant backing of all that I do. Thank you for bringing me in to be a part of the Leaf family and making room for me even when I leave at the drop of a hat to catch the next flight to LA. Your encouragement and the stability you have provided for me in Liverpool has abundantly blessed me.

My list of thanks could continue for hours but I want to honour those men and women who have endorsed this book and personally stood by me. Thank you to Shawn Bolz for believing in me and in the words penned in this book; to Cheryl Allen for welcoming me into the PIHOP family and seeking to see me released further; to Annie Dieselberg, Celeste McGee and Andréa Vargas for letting my journey interact with theirs and opening my eyes wider to the immense power, beauty and responsibility we have to love.

My heart is full when I think on these things and see these faces in my mind. From the bottom of my heart, thank you.

Contents

I write this book in dedication to every pearl that I have encountered, those moments of getting to look deep into your eyes and hear the stories of your heart will stay with me for eternity. In particular this book is written in honour of Kerrie Higgins who passed away in January 2012, your light is still shining so bright.

Soi 4

I want you to take a moment to walk with me into Nana Plaza, the headquarters of the red-light district in Bangkok. Imagine a courtyard area built up on each side by three-storeys worth of strip bars and clubs. All of your senses are immediately hit as you walk in from Soi 4, a street that is lined with pubs and bars to attract its foreign clientele. Street vendors crowd into the plaza's entrance, the smell of chicken and mangos mingle to meet your nostrils; the pavements are packed with sex workers and foreigners, beggars dotted in-between. As you walk into the plaza your vision is immediately overwhelmed with the sight of neon lights, scantily dressed men and women and hoards of (rarely sober) western men. Music is blaring from every club entrance and the sound of men smacking signs to try to get your attention fills your ears.

The 'entertainment' that Nana Plaza offers you ranges from underage girls, ladyboys, ping-pong shows and sadomasochism. Once you've chosen your destination and entered the bar you get seated by one of the servers on benches or booths that line the walls of the room, often three seats deep. In the centre of the room is a stage with several poles where the men or women will dance. There are mirrors everywhere so that no matter where you look you encounter your surroundings.

Every worker has a number pinned to them and that is their identity in this world: a number. If a customer likes the look of a particular number then he can get them added to the drinks bill and leave with them, like choosing from a menu.

Welcome to Nana Plaza, where lust is the number one priority.

This is where I spent a beautiful and heartbreaking two weeks in January 2012 with a team of new friends from California, USA. We were travelling under the banner of Tapestry International, a non-profit organization whose vision is to build transforming communities and to renew individuals around the world, by serving, training and empowering indigenous leaders and non-profit organizations that work in areas of injustice. I had encountered Tapestry through my church community in Los Angeles which was called Expression 58, and it was here that I met Annie Zirbel who was the leader of this trip to Bangkok.

I once met a lady whose business card read 'International Treasure Hunter'. That title struck me because I realized that this is a part of God's calling for my life – to find his beautiful, lost treasure. Purity is a treasure that often gets mislaid, overlooked or left unwanted but actually I believe it is one of the most precious of jewels. It can often be found in the most unlikely of places, or at other times it can feel like you're grappling in the dark to maintain its presence.

On 25 January 2012 I wrote the following in my journal:

Slavery has never felt so real.

We ate dinner in a restaurant where trafficked women from Uzbekistan live and work. We watched them get ready for the night whilst we ate beef and rice. They looked at us with hard and broken eyes.

Then we truly entered hell.

Splitting into two teams of five we headed out to the bars at Nana. Our first stop was Angelwitch.

As soon as I stepped inside, the heaviness of the oppression in the room hit me. There were a lot of customers already and even more women working. We got seated at the back of the room next to a young white couple who were there enjoying the show together. There were a few small clusters of men and several guys sat on their own accompanied by a Thai woman. The stage was full of women all wearing black bondage gear and leather boots. Once on stage they would pull back the bits of material covering their breasts and begin dancing bare-chested.

The Mama-san (the lady who is basically in charge of the bar) was freaking out that we had been allowed in and began performing rituals against us from the other side of the room. I caught a girl's eye on stage and she immediately put on the face of seduction.

I was finding it increasingly hard to know how to operate in this place where everything smelt of death and seduction. I wanted out of there so badly but instead I sat and observed from my punter's seat . . .

One of the crazy things about the show was that so much of the music reminded me of Disneyland. You are about to watch the Disneyland of sexual fantasy. My stomach felt a new level of sickness as I battled with what was being shown on stage.

Some of the women looked so dead. You looked at their eyes and just received a blank gaze. They were performing in the flesh but they had taken themselves elsewhere.

I think the show lasted for about half an hour and I literally let out a sigh of relief when it was all over. There was one performance that I think will stay with me for a long time as two women acted out a massage parlour scene. They both ended up completely naked as one girl massaged the other. The men watching were captivated, almost drooling at what they saw. The women on stage were beautiful but empty. I don't think I will ever forget one woman's face as she went through the motions of massaging her friend. Her eyes were lifeless. I can't imagine what it must feel like to be placed in such a demeaning position; naked, completely vulnerable, performing a sexual act with your friend on a stage in front of many gawking men. What does that do to your precious heart?

Angelwitch broke my heart.

Another performance involved audience participation so a guy got pulled up onstage and given a pretty intense lap dance. He sat in that chair wearing a wedding ring. Then the women were herded back onstage again and the meat market resumed. We left and it was immediately easier to breathe.

I share that experience with you because as I sat in that big red booth I had to really fight for purity, to hear its voice and feel its presence. The air was thick with temptations that whispered and tugged at every part of me, leaving me with a sense of powerlessness against the spiritual inhabitants of the room. I tried to focus on the name of Jesus, the purest name that I knew, repeating it over and over in my head. However, I found that two-syllable name constantly being sucked from my lips and I had to keep pulling my mind back into line with his name. And yet I did find his presence. Surrounded by so many elements of darkness I was still able to recognize that God was with me and experienced moments of peace that washed over me and enabled me to remain in my seat. It didn't take away from the intense oppression in the room but it was a subtle reminder that my God is still bigger than the darkness.

You may be tempted to ask what the point of all this was. Why did we stay in such a place? I realized afterwards that it was to simply be. Our mission that night was not to go in guns blazing, shouting 'thou shalt nots' at people. Our mission was to affect the atmosphere.

We are all carriers of an atmosphere: a presence that affects whatever environment we step into. On our bad days we can easily affect those around us with our negative emotional pile up, just as easily as it is possible to shift someone else's raincloud with our beaming smiles and rays of hope. We are all atmosphere changers whether for good or bad and that night in Angelwitch served the purpose of bringing light into darkness. This could be clearly seen from the Mama-san who was sending curses our way, to the odd looks we got from those around us. We did nothing to attract attention to ourselves, we were just present. Present in a place where the things of darkness were celebrated and worshipped and light is not often found. But darkness always recognizes Jesus' Light and it has no choice but to bow to it.

For many of us the idea of going into places such as Angelwitch can seem overwhelming, fill us with fear or just make us very uncomfortable. The first time I walked into the courtyard of

Nana Plaza I was overcome with a feeling of sickness and had to resist the strong urge to run out and back to the safety of our hotel. At moments like these the darkness can seem so much stronger and in control than the little tea light we seem to be holding in our hands. And yes, in some places we enter, the darkness is well established, but it doesn't make us weaker. We are light-carriers, illuminators of darkness, and we always win. Victory isn't about winning the lottery or establishing a successful business, it isn't even about having a beautiful home and loving family, it is about seeing godly characteristics and principles being restored to our world and lives. This looks like a display of love to a woman that has only ever been used; it is seeing freedom and the restoration of justice to those that have been subjected to torture and discrimination by others; it is letting peace be our anthem and joy our foundation as we go about our day-to-day routines. On many occasions it can seem like we are losing battle after battle, however ultimately it is the light that always extinguishes darkness and good that always overcomes evil.

In a world like Nana Plaza, I found myself encountering various degrees of spiritual and emotional darkness. I know that those who are in charge of Angelwitch do not worship the same God as me, who I would describe as exuding light and freedom, but instead perform daily rituals to gods who rule by fear and control. As soon as we walked into that bar, we walked into territory that felt in blatant opposition to the freedom that I know and live by.

Outside every bar, store and house in Bangkok can be found a spirit house where offerings are left daily to appease their gods. It's impossible not to consider the issue of spirituality as everywhere and everyone displays which deity they believe in and worship. It is shown in the tattoos that many Thai people have on their backs, or the idols that are sold in every street market. The concept of religion isn't just about whether or not you go to church on a Sunday, it is literally felt in the warm air around you as you behold a culture's respect for powers that are greater than theirs. Conflict between spiritual freedom and control is a reality you can't escape from and therefore it's not a surprise if you're not welcomed with open arms into every place that you enter. I know that the rituals that are performed in Angelwitch each night are of a much more intense nature than most of the other bars that we went into and therefore create an atmosphere that is completely the opposite of the one carried by my friends and me. The greeting we received there was a lot more hostile than other places simply because there was no openness to what we represented and believed in.

Another bar that we went into during our time in Bangkok, and in which we actually became regulars, was a ladyboy bar situated on the second floor of Nana Plaza. By the last time that we visited the workers there, the Mama-san was stood waiting outside the entrance and opened her arms wide to embrace us when she saw us coming. Such a different welcome from that which we had received in Angelwitch!

Each night we would sit and buy the men and women drinks and talk to them, being clear that we weren't there for their services, but just to listen. They were very open to telling us their stories, how they had ended up in Bangkok, what their dreams for the future were. By the last night I think the ladyboys knew that we were there because of love, even if they did not understand what this meant. There are now people regularly visiting that bar, from the non-profit organizations that we were working with, continuing to build relationships both with the ladyboys and the Mama-san.

It's a challenge to know how to act and what to say when you are sat in a strip bar next to a man who looks more feminine than some of the women you know, but it's a challenge I found great joy in accepting. In choosing to look them straight in the eyes, not focusing on their raunchy attire or rising to their flirtatious behaviour, I found a love pouring out of me that was beyond my mortal means. Love has to be our anthem. It has to be that which gives us vision, that which sends us, and that which upholds us.

So there we were in the humidity of Thailand's capital: seven westerners who had a huge desire for justice and to love society's unlovable. Our time had been moulded into a tight schedule of working between NightLight, an international organization that is committed to addressing the complex issues of commercial sexual exploitation through prevention, intervention, restoration and education, and Dton Naam Ministries, a non-profit charity and foundation that helps individuals leave prostitution and find healing physically, emotionally and spiritually. Some days would find us doing back-to-back prayer ministry with men and women who used to work in the sex trade or were transitioning out. Other days we would find ourselves doing basic teaching sessions in art, business and photography. Most nights you could also find us in Nana Plaza doing bar outreach to the men and women working in the bars there.

When we arrived as a team we didn't have much idea of what we'd be doing, but we soon discovered that we would be stretched in ways we weren't expecting. One of these occasions occurred during our time working with NightLight. Every morning the women who work for NightLight gather for about an hour where they sing worship songs and hear a short talk from one of the staff members: a beautiful way to start a working day. As the visiting team of eager volunteers, we were asked to lead one of these morning sessions. Now, given the choice between either speaking or singing I would choose speaking every time: I'm comfortable with words and have had plenty of practise in communicating over the last few years. However, this time I found myself in a little makeshift worship team as a vocalist and leading a couple of the songs . . . cue a stomach full of butterflies! Without even having time to practice, Joel, Annie and I led a group of about sixty Night-Light workers in worship that morning and it honestly felt quite glorious: I could feel the presence of God enveloping the room in such a beautiful, pure way that didn't have so much to do with our playing or singing but more the desire to worship him with what we had, however great or little that was.

There is something that happens in those moments of quiet obedience, when you silence the voice of fear that tells you that you are not qualified, and you follow the gentle prodding that suggests that potentially something glorious could occur if you step over that line of comfort . . . you encounter the gift of beauty.

Throughout our time in Bangkok I came across that quality in the most unlikely of places as I befriended sex tourists and sex workers alike. Beauty doesn't bow down to what's appropriate: it appears where there is even a sliver of purity.

18 January 2012

Day one is over and settling in to sleep. I actually now feel strangely at home here. Until this evening I had it in my mind that everything is super intense and so was walking around feeling kind of guarded. And yes it is intense, but there is also so much love to be found here.

Before dinner we went to one of NightLight's buildings which is just around the corner from Nana Plaza. We then spent about an hour worshipping and that's what brought down the guard in my heart. I began to see love pouring out of the eyes of Jesus directed to everyone passing by our shop front window. And the eyes of Jesus were us. Love, joy and a peace about being here, in this environment, enveloped me.

One of my favourite encounters with purity occurred during one of our last nights of outreach into the Nana Plaza area. I was paired up with one of my team members, Carly, and we made our way to the third floor of the plaza to a bar called Las Vegas. It was here that we saw girls as young as 16 working amongst the older women. They were so young, so beautiful, and so vulnerable.

Carly and I stayed in this bar for a while before leaving and making our way downstairs to the ground floor and trying to decide what was right to do next. As we wound our way through the outside bar in the middle of the plaza, we passed a group of white lads, one of whom started to hit on me. I ignored him and carried on walking, trying to settle my stomach again. There is something really sickening about someone chatting you up in this environment.

We both stopped near the entrance to the plaza and were talking about where to go when a guy appeared at my left side and greeted me with a big hello. I was expecting it to be the lad that we had just passed, so I turned towards him with my cold expression ready when I realized that I already knew this man.

The previous Sunday our whole team had been given the day off to relax and recoup. I decided that I wanted to go for a wander and so left our hotel with one of my American friends, Dave. We'd been walking through the local markets talking for a little while when a tuk tuk (a typical Thailand taxi) driver called out to us and offered us a tour of the city. We politely said no and carried on away from him. A little later we were retracing our steps when we again saw him, running up to us and drawing out a map of where he could take us in the city for just 20 baht. We conceded and jumped in.

We'd been driving around for about ten minutes when our driver stopped and told us to get out and go into this store while he got gas. Neither Dave nor I had a clue where we were or quite what was going on but we obediently went into the tailor's store. As soon as we entered, a group of Indian men came out of the back and ushered us further into the store to show us their wares. At this point Dave started to freak out and thought we were about to be trafficked, saying: 'What's going on? Where are you taking us?' I found myself trying to calm Dave and reassure him that we weren't about to get trafficked and everything was going to be fine, whilst also finding the whole thing very funny.

It turned out we weren't the only slightly bewildered westerners in the store at that moment, as at the back of the shop was an Australian guy trying to turn down the offer of a new suit. I got chatting to him and found out that he had just arrived in the country that morning on a business trip and now had no real idea of what was going on.

We all ended up leaving the store at the same time and rejoining our respective tuk tuk drivers to re-embark on our little adventure. Throughout the rest of our tour we kept passing our new Australian friend who would merrily wave and shout out where he was off to next. I loved this whole experience although by the end of it I don't think Dave's nerves could take another stop, as he was convinced we were seconds away from being abducted by some crazy traffickers!

So now fast forward again to me and Carly stood in the middle of Nana Plaza with a smiling white man who showed signs of intoxication and who I sensed didn't belong there. It was my Australian tuk tuk friend. As we talked for the few minutes that followed, and I observed the way he looked around our surroundings, it became obvious to me that this man wasn't your normal hungry punter. His eyes were kind and warm and, although I could tell he was curious, my instincts as a woman told me that I could trust him, he just needed to be reminded of what was real. The world that is displayed in Nana Plaza isn't reality; it is nothing more than fantasy.

At this point I would like to say that Nana is somewhere that you don't expect to meet someone that you know – or at least you really pray that you don't. There had been several times when we had passed guys in this area and I had done a double-take as, for a split second, a face had looked familiar. Thankfully I was always wrong.

My internal thought processes quickly caught up to the present situation and I began to engage in conversation, covering up my surprise and sadness to see him in such a place. He seemed equally surprised to see me and asked what I was doing out here. 'We have friends who work in the bars here so we've come to visit the girls and buy them a drink. What are you doing here?' It really does take some skill to try to have a normal conversation in the centre of Bangkok's internationally known sex industry . . .

'I've been out with some friends from work and now I'm here getting a drink.'

'Oh cool . . . so how do you find it here . . . honestly?' I found myself asking him directly, making it clear that I didn't like anything about our surroundings. He looked around us as he began to answer and I could tell that the reality of where he was had started to seep back into his vision.

'Well . . . it is pretty crazy, isn't it?'

'Yes it is. It's crazy that sex is nothing more than a menu here.'

Our conversation continued on for a bit and then we parted ways. I was hesitant to let him go as I found myself wanting to bring him out of that place and back to where he belonged. He didn't belong there. But I had to let him go; I had done my part in that brief encounter: I had reminded him of purity. Sometimes our presence is more powerful than our words. It impacts beyond knowledge and speaks to the soul.

If I speak in the tongues of men or of angels, but do not have love, I am only a resounding gong or a clanging cymbal.
(1 Corinthians 13:1)

Pearls:

Poppy

Pearls can be found whenever we choose to open our eyes. They are hidden in the gutters and alleyways, they are propped up in bus shelters and they appear on our way to work. Pearls are too precious to be ignored or walked past, they deserve attention and care; to be washed and cleaned, removed of all dirt and grime and set in a bed of soft velvet. They are created in conflict and friction, in dark, closed and protected places but that only adds to their value.

Again, the kingdom of heaven is like a merchant looking for
fine pearls. When he found one of great value, he went away
and sold everything he had and bought it.
(Matthew 13:45,46)

'Do you have a boyfriend?' I was asked by a young girl with beautiful brown eyes who was carefully painting my nails a pale shade of pink.

'I don't have a boyfriend right now: I broke up with someone a little while ago.'

'Oh okay.' She carried on carefully applying the nail varnish.

'Do you have a boyfriend?' I asked gently, not wanting to upset the balance of this precious moment.

'I did have one, that's how I ended up coming to England.' She spoke without missing a stroke of the varnish brush. 'He was my boyfriend at home and he invited me to come to England with him to meet his friends because he had work here. My parents let me come because he was nice to me and we were happy together. Then he introduced me to his friends and took me visiting different places. Things changed then and he wasn't always nice to me anymore and I was made to do things with him and the men. I'm living here now to be safe and the people here are trying to help me get back to my country.'

She spoke as if all she was talking about was the weather or a holiday that she had been on that summer, her tone denying the grim truth that her reason for being in the UK was that she had been trafficked for sexual exploitation. My heart broke within me as I listened, feeling completely helpless to do anything but show her that I cared and had time for her. I wanted to throw my arms around her and tell her over and over again how precious and beautiful she is, how she deserved so much more than what had been done to her, that things would get better and her heart would one day feel healed and restored. It was like my insides were melting in response to her story and a prayer began to be silently lifted toward heaven.

God, where is your justice? Let your justice flow!
How do you want me to respond to this beautiful heart?
What am I meant to do when this injustice feels so overwhelming?
God, I need you, we need you. We need your justice!

'Do you miss your family?' I found the conversation continuing regardless of my inner cries to the skies.

'Yes I do, but I think it's going to be a while before I can go home again because it's not safe. While I'm waiting, I'm finding happiness here.' I was stunned as I listened to her talk and I watched her calmness as she went about her work. I had read so much about trafficking, had thoroughly done my research and exposed myself to the horrendous truth of its meaning, but all of those words seemed to disappear in the presence of a beautiful young girl who brought the dictionary definition to life.

We met in a safe house in England where I had come to visit on an afternoon that hosted a pamper session for the girls. I was meant to be offering hand massages and manicures to the women who came but here I was being loved by the one whom I had come to love. I found myself humbled, not knowing how to respond except that I shouldn't get up.

> *He has shown you, O mortal, what is good.*
> *And what does the LORD require of you?*
> *To act justly and to love mercy*
> *and to walk humbly with your God.*
> *(Micah 6:8)*

There have been many times when I've thought that I've figured it out. I've known the facts and the figures, what the problem was and what changes were needed to bring about a solution. Then I meet someone and I listen to their story with them for a long or short time and my heart is humbled. This journey of seeking beauty and justice is not a maths equation ending in a nice whole number, it is a surrendered walk with love that ends in an embrace with pure joy.

Poppy was 16 years old when I met her. She had entered the UK at the age of 15 as a victim of human trafficking. Thankfully she was rescued and her life began to be reshaped by people who loved her, were for her and sought to protect and not to harm her. She was the first pearl that I got to sit with and hear her story and she is one that I will never forget.

2

Dear Hub

'Sex is great! Sex is great!' I found myself stood in a large room with between fifty to seventy other young people chanting this slogan, watching a couple of very excited Americans leading everyone on stage. These were the moments running up to receiving my medal of purity, a silver ring that would remain on my finger until my future wedding day.

My young 15-year-old self eagerly took in everything that they were saying, through the media presentations and short talks that communicated God's desire for purity within sex and relationships. The aim of the evening was to give every young person present a fresh perspective on sex: that it is amazing and is designed to unite a couple within marriage and not to just be given away to anyone who desires it. The young people at the event were a mixture of Christians and non-Christian kids, some of whom no doubt thought that Christians probably didn't approve of sex, so the audience's chant was a great way to kill that thought. I already knew what my decision would be before the event began and was looking forward to taking my declaration of purity, standing with my younger brother, Peter and close friend, Sarah.

It was three rather excited and impassioned teenagers that my dad had the pleasure of driving back up to Stoke-on-Trent that night, with moments of quiet overtaking us from time to time as we thought of who we might be wearing these rings for.

Excerpt from the 'Hub journals':

10 June 2004

Dear Hub,

I guess the next major thing to tell you actually involves you. On 26 June 2004 I went to Birmingham with my dad, brother Peter, and Sarah, to the Silver Ring Thing. That night I made a pledge to you and to everyone around me that I will keep my virginity till my wedding night, to give to you as a gift. As a token of that pledge to you, I received a silver ring. Every time I look at that ring I think of you. I wonder what you're up to and how you are. I smile because I love you and I can't wait for the future, to spend it with you. I want to give you all of me, not just a part.

Hub became the name of affection that I gave to the mystery man who I would one day marry, and soon after the pledge I began writing to him. I wanted him to be a part of my life even if he wasn't physically around yet and so began writing in my journal to him, recording both the big and little happenings of my life. Wherever I went my journals would travel with me and soon became well known by my close friends as we talked and wondered about who our 'Hubs' might be!

I've always been a lover of books and as a child I would often be found in some 'secret' corner of the house, curled up with a good novel. I say secret, as to me they were: little spaces of quiet sanctuary where I could pretend that I was in another world and no one could really see me. In reality though I'm pretty sure they were very obvious to the adults in the house but they were very good at indulging my imagination. I grew to love this romanticized idea of writing diaries that would one day be found by someone else and would reveal beautiful stories of love and loss. Yes, I've always been a bit of a dreamer!

The plan was that I would write to Hub from the time of the pledge until our wedding day, then give the journals to him as a gift on our wedding night; a giving of my past to my future. So, full of girlish dreams of what was yet to come, on the night of the pledge, I said yes, put on my ring and began the adventure of finding Hub.

Within a week of receiving our silver rings, Peter and I ended up in the local paper where they produced a double-page spread on our decision to stand for purity. Something that had started as a personal choice became a public declaration: a foretaste of my journey to come.

When I look back on the last thirteen years I can see clearly how God called me from a young age to be set apart for him. He placed in me a desire for purity that was fiery and passionate. I can also see how the area of purity then became my biggest battlefield and area of pain, although I wouldn't trade my journey for anything.

Purity is generally defined as freedom from any contaminant, or guilt, or evil; a state of innocence.

The power of purity is often underestimated, trampled upon or overlooked in today's society. We care more about instant pleasure and maintaining beauty and appearances than protecting the purity and innocence of our hearts and minds. Our value system looks down upon youth and frowns at it as immature but praises those who take on adulthood before their time. Freedom is associated with age in the mind of a young person and they scramble to add the years on to their timeline.

Sexual purity is also often a subject that seems to be hemmed into a timeframe allocated to teenagers and the thinking seems to be that once we break free from those teen years we don't need to talk about it so much anymore. The truth is that no matter how old we are, whether we are single, married, dating or divorced there is always a conversation to be had about purity. The battle for purity isn't just for the single: it doesn't end when you get a ring on your finger or say, 'I do.' It may get easier in some areas but the temptation can just begin to look different. We are all called to be pure, to live in purity and to love purely.

It is God's will that you should be sanctified: that you should
avoid sexual immorality
(1 Thessalonians 4:3)

It's not as simple as just wearing a ring: that isn't what secures your purity. Purity isn't about simply abstaining from sex; it's about maintaining honour and integrity in thought, word and deed. It's not about how much you can push a boundary but about how far back from a boundary line you can stand.

From Genesis to Revelation flows a story about purity. At times it might seem lost amongst the drama of war stories and humanity's failed attempts to get things right, but a reminder can always be found: a subtle hint that above all else God desires a pure heart and a life that is devoted to him. Purity is not an idea to be bypassed but rather one to camp out in, study and put into practice. It is a key that unlocks favour and honour, and reveals the treasures of the kingdom of heaven. It is a continuous journey that is strengthened in community and accountability, and is overflowing in promises.

> *Joshua told the people, 'Consecrate yourselves, for tomorrow the*
> Lord *will do amazing things among you.'*
> (Joshua 3:5)

The verse says 'will': there is no 'maybe', 'if' or 'potentially'. God promises to answer our pure hearts with his goodness, his might and his wonder. Whenever I have chosen purity over the other options laid before me, I've always been amazed at how God has honoured that and responded with nothing other than his goodness. I want my life to produce miracles; I want my legacy to be purity. I don't want to fall prey again to the cheap replicas of love and intimacy that Satan offers.

So at the age of 15 my choice was verbalized: to choose a life of sexual purity, whether single, dating or married; that my body and relationships would bring honour to my God. I wore my silver ring with pride and confidence following that June night, then a couple of months later lost it on Fistral beach in Cornwall during my first time surfing. I was honestly quite distraught at the time and soon invested in another one, this time purchasing one from the jewellery section in Argos. Over the following twelve months I gradually stopped wearing a ring altogether, not through a desire to back out of my pledge but more through a tendency to keep losing the ring!

I wonder now whether my simple struggles to keep hold of the ring were a prophetic sign of the battle to maintain purity that I would find myself in. Maybe it's just a picture of another young teenager who has a problem with forget-fulness. Whatever the conclusion, that year did spark the beginnings of a much more real fight to keep a lifestyle of consecration.

If you were to read through my journals from 2004–05 you would find dramatic entry after entry as I found myself 'in love', wondering if every boy I liked was Hub and encoun-tering option after option as more of the world was exposed to me. I really did think I'd found Hub at one point and would constantly remind my parents that I could get married at 16 with their permission. I can only say that I am glad that I didn't!

The best way to describe that time is that it was like being in a tug of war and I was the rope. There were countless occasions where I would find real clarity in the things that I was facing: I knew what the right thing to do was and I could hear God clearly speaking to me. But seemingly within moments of those revelations I would find myself confused and falling for the words of affirmation that were being offered to me from all the wrong sources, and more often than not I found myself compromising my faith and desire for a lifestyle of purity. I never had sex with anyone but I did give my heart away to people who didn't know how to care for it. In not knowing how to care for my heart I therefore gave permis-sion for others to enter who were just as inexperienced. I was hungry to be found beautiful, to be wanted, to be loved: all desires that can easily be read by others who carry the same. They attract each other.

Maybe you can blame this season on the fact that I was a teenager and faced the kinds of issues that every teenager has to face. I do believe that there was more going on though than just my age. I believe in the natural realm that we can all see and all inhabit, but I also believe in the supernatural realm that we don't always have the eyes to see but is just as active and present. The presence of good also implies that there is an opposite force: evil. I know that the pledge I took in June 2004 was a stand that I chose, not just for myself, but for the kingdom of heaven. I hadn't really prepared myself though for the fact that I might have to fight hard to maintain it.

For a while, starting in the spring of 2005, I flirted with a relationship with an older guy whom I knew and who didn't believe in the same things as me. Although I think he genuinely did care for me, he didn't know how to honour me. I found myself caught up in something that had won me emotionally, feeding the needs I had, but which began to tear at my spirit. As I managed to come out of that cycle of seeing him, telling him I couldn't see him and seeing him again, I could see the unhealthy forces that were driving his actions. He was addicted to pornography and his vision was filled with lust, not a desire for purity. Where my vision had been filled with a desire for consecration, as I became emotionally tied to him, his vision began to infiltrate mine. I found myself being the object of his fantasies and reduced to an object in his mind.

What we fill our eyes with will ultimately affect our actions and the way we are able to love. A fantasy-filled vision loves the encounter more than the journey and as long as it is focusing on unreality will be unable to truly hold another's heart with honour. The vision that locks eyes with purity values the growth and beauty of the other over a fleeting dance with lust.

6 June 2005

Dear Hub,

He asked me out tonight and I said yes. Maybe he is you and he just needs my help to get saved. I dunno. I'm tired of trying to work it all out in my head, will just see what happens.

The choices I made in those months, to allow my heart to be connected with his, ended up following me for years to come. I let myself believe the lie that I could change him and save him, and that I wouldn't be affected at all. The problem was that his resolve to have me was stronger than mine to save him. The relationship didn't last long and was frowned upon by everyone I told but unfortunately the damage had already been done.

For several years I believed that how I had been treated by him was normal, that I was nothing more than an object that could be called upon and used for another's fulfilment. Again, sexually nothing ever happened, but emotionally and psychologically a lot had been instilled in a short amount of time. Of course there was a foundation of insecurity in me already that this experience built upon, and had been formed from previous years and encounters, but I want to highlight how one's sexual brokenness can inform another's without any intention to do so.

Women were not created just for man's gain and pleasure, neither were men just created to fulfil a woman's desire. We were created to complement the other in honour, integrity and love; to hold each other's hearts in purity and create an environment within relationship where they are released to be all that they were made to be, to reach the fullness of their potential and destiny. Neither man nor woman is an object: they are a being; a loving, breathing, beautiful being.

It is now my aim in life to love well: to honour those I encounter, and to choose a lifestyle of purity even if that means personal sacrifice. It is not a path that is easily trodden and increasingly goes against the grain of western society, often involving making decisions that seem so alien to many people. Choosing a lifestyle that is set apart from the norm has been challenging, and I've not always got it right, but I have found freedom and a wholeness of heart that has only ever escaped me when I've tried to do things the world's way.

3

An Education

'Mum, have you seen my phone?' I stood in the living room doorway, an agitated tone filtering into my question and a rising anger in my chest at the possibility of what the answer might be. 'Where did you last have it, love?' 'I left it on the desk in the dining room and now it's gone.' Mum got up, frowning, and followed me into the other room where we began searching through the other objects that had found their home on the old wooden desk. 'Do you think Val might have taken it?' I was the first one to let the question spill out that had clearly been on both of our minds. Any amount of grace that I had been feeling an hour earlier was quickly waning away. 'It's very possible love, she has taken things from me before now if I've left them lying around. I'm sorry, I tried to make sure she wasn't left on her own at all in here . . . it's definitely not in your room?' If there's one thing a teenager knows, it's where they last put their mobile phone: 'I'm sure, Mum, I left it in here when I went upstairs. I thought it would be safe!' I was mad now with the sort of anger that blurs your vision slightly, causing all of the wrong words and actions to crash out of you.

Val was a woman that our family had become well acquainted with over the past few months and was well known in our neighbourhood for her line of work. Roughly every other Saturday my mum would go out with one of her friends to visit the street sex workers who could be found quite easily in our area. Val was one of the women whom my mum had got to know well and every now and then, along with a few other women, she would call round to our house seeking help. Today was one of those days.

Four out of my five siblings and I were being taught at home at this point and had just finished our lunch together when Val called around. Soon after her arrival we all vacated the downstairs to our various rooms, wanting to avoid getting caught up in anything messy. I tended not to be the biggest fan of some of the visitors we had calling round to our house. I could see their obvious need for help and their genuine love for my mum but then their addictions would speak, overtaking truth and spelling out lies in their attempts to get what they wanted. It seemed to me that at times they would try to take advantage of my mum, which caused an element of resentment to settle in my heart.

Now, stood in the dining room realizing that Val had probably stolen my new phone, I felt a surge of anger at this injustice. She only lived a few doors down, at the bottom of our street, and in that moment I decided I was going to confront her. I felt a determination that I've later learnt comes from my hatred for injustice: I soon found myself marching down the street to Val's house.

I stood outside the white door and knocked firmly, the ball of upset and anger causing my stomach to churn. After a second knock it opened to reveal Tom, the pimp who resided there, looking a little surprised to see me but smiling nonetheless. 'Is

Val here?' I looked at him straight in the eyes, giving no room for any attempt at lies. 'Yeah . . . she's in her room. I don't think she's able to take visitors though.' 'She took my phone and I'm here to get it back please.' I was determined to get what I came for and, after looking at me for a second, Tom let me in. 'I'm not sure she has your phone anymore, babe, but you can go up and speak to her if you like,' Tom pointed up the stairs, directing me to the right.

I began making my way up the steep staircase, in a house that had seen better days, still too fired up to really think about where I was and the surroundings in which I now found myself. I followed the narrow corridor round to the right, past a closed door, to a bedroom with a door that stood slightly ajar. I opened it to find Val sprawled on the bed as if she'd been thrown there by some mightier force and hadn't found the strength to move herself since. Her head was half propped up on the wall that the bed was against, her mouth partly open and what I could see of her eyes revealed emptiness and disconnection. I stood there for a few seconds suddenly unsure what to do. The room itself was small and unkempt, the evidence of drugs and alcohol strewn on the floor.

'Val, I'd like my phone back, please. I know you've taken it.' I addressed the lifeless form on the bed, my voice sounding quite pitiful against its harsh surroundings. A murmur came from the open mouth and Val stirred in my direction, trying to focus her eyes on me. 'I don't have your phone.' 'She sold it already, babe, to get that hit.' Tom appeared at my side, 'I'm sorry.' He turned to go back downstairs, signalling for me to do the same. I looked again at Val: a mixture of pity, anger and upset surging through me and briefly disabling any movement, before also turning, following Tom back down the stairs. I could feel the hurt stinging at my heart as I walked back up the street to my own home, angry questions steam-rollering through my mind, and at the same time the image of Val planted firmly in my memory.

My years living in Cobridge, the red-light district of Stoke-on-Trent, became my introduction to the part of society that most of us would rather not have to acknowledge exists. I was definitely one of the more reluctant members of our family to move from the quiet suburban area that we had been residing in, to 'the heart of the Potteries', where we felt God was now calling us to live. Following that incident with Val I also made a firm decision that I would never work with sex workers or those struggling with addictions: it was definitely not for me.

Cobridge is situated just outside Hanley, which operates as Stoke-on-Trent's main city centre, and is an area mostly populated with ethnic minorities as well as having a large percentage of broken families. Racial tensions would arise from time to time, mainly between the large groups of young Pakistani people and the white families in the area: it was never a one-sided fight. Crime happened, as it does in every area, but in an area like Cobridge it tends to be less hidden and more talked about. We became a well-respected and loved family in our time there and although that didn't keep us entirely separate from trouble, we did experience some degree of safety.

I now consider it a privilege to have been able to live in an area like Cobridge and have gradually become a lot less bothered if my street is a little rough around the edges. We all want to live in safety, but sometimes God asks us to live in the discomfort of brokenness and welcome others into the sanctuary that we know and call home.

After the phone incident occurred with Val, our family became good friends with Tom and he later started coming to our church and made a decision to become a Christian. He is now happily married and lives a life far removed from the one in which we first encountered him. Val also continued to have a close relationship with my mum although unfortunately a few years later she passed away after an accidental drug overdose. I watched many lives get radically touched through my parents and their choice to do life in an area that many would avoid; I will always honour them for that.

One of the individuals who was befriended by my parents was a West Indian woman in her fifties who lived in one of the houses that backed onto ours. Lisa came from a large family and was related to one of the main drug dealers in the area. Although full of needs and battling with bipolar disorder, she was a very lovable character once you got to know her and would regularly come by for a cup of tea or to borrow a fiver. She was also impacted by my parents' faith and later they were able to witness her being baptized at a local church.

It wasn't unusual for Lisa to lock herself out of her house and my dad became quite the expert in breaking in for her. There aren't many men in their forties that I can think of who would be able to climb through the narrow window of a terraced house, but this was just another day in Cobridge for my dad!

Towards the end of my thirteenth year I became a paper-girl, twice a day delivering newspapers to our area. Some days it would be a rather enjoyable task and I would quite happily bounce through the streets, often in my own little world as I delved into my imagination. Then there would be those days in winter where it would literally take every bit of willpower I had to get myself round to the little newsagents and pick up my bag of papers for delivery. Countless times I remember coming home completely drenched, my legs weighed down by baggy jeans that had soaked up half a cloud of rain. I learnt a lot in those years as a papergirl though, both in how to be a good employee and how to look after myself.

One sunny Sunday morning I was happily doing my usual paper delivery route, looking forward to the church service that we would be attending as a family, when a silver car slowed down just ahead of me on the opposite side of the road. The driver wound down his window, trying to get my attention. I was on a main road and had just left the premises of a BUPA care home. No one else was around as I warily came to a halt to hear what he had to say.

The driver was an older man with greying hair. His eyes were bloodshot and he looked potentially drunk. Words were tumbling out of his mouth but I couldn't understand them and moved off the pavement into the road to try to hear better. A couple of other cars arrived on the scene, forcing me back onto the pavement and in response the silver car then swung itself around to join me on my side of the road. Thinking that he was after directions I walked up to the car window to try to make sense of the man's words. 'Are you open for business?' He leaned out of his window towards me, an air of impatience around him. 'Business?' I was confused. 'Yes, well, I'm delivering papers.' I had no idea what 'business' meant but thought it might be a foreign way of asking for a *Sunday*

Mail. 'You know . . . business . . . you come with me and I'll pay you. I'll give you £20.' The cloud of confusion was quickly parting from around my head and I began backing away from the car. 'No, no I don't do that sort of business.' I began to feel sick and afraid. 'Come on, £20, I'll pay you £20!' he said aggressively. His bloodshot eyes were fixed on me in a way that demanded I say yes. 'No!' I was walking away from the car now, as fast as I could back up the road. I had quickly begun to feel panicky and tearful. The silver car hadn't disappeared like I had hoped: I could see it in my peripheral vision creeping up beside me. I tried to ignore it by walking faster but the car's engine matched my speed and the driver repeated his question.

'If I can just make it to the junction it'll be alright.' The thought began to play through my mind as I focused on the traffic lights coming up ahead that connected my road with the busy main one that ran through Cobridge. The lights became my goalpost and I tried to ignore the voice and the thought of the man with the bloodshot eyes. I reached the lights before he did, thankful for the other vehicles that were now around me, and waited for the little green man to allow me to cross the street and get away from the silver car. An aggressive voice reached me first though as his car came past me, the window still down and an arm reaching out in a vain attempt to grasp me. I couldn't decipher much of what he said apart from the repetition of '£20'! He then suddenly sped off and I watched as our encounter came to an end.

I was shaking for the remainder of my delivery route, my mind working in overtime as I processed what had just taken place and the disgusting feeling that I had at the thought of someone offering me money to sleep with them. I breathed an inward sigh of relief when I finally made it safely back home and ate my breakfast in silence before changing out of the jeans and red sweater that I had previously felt so comfortable in.

Before leaving for church I managed to shake off the feeling of shame that had begun to sink in and opened up to my parents about what had happened. I've never particularly enjoyed having those sorts of conversations with my mum and dad: the kind where you can see the pain they feel as they look at you and feel their fierce protection as they hold you and comfort you. These moments with those that we love, I've now discovered, are unavoidable when choosing to live a lifestyle of vulnerability.

That morning I spoke to my youth pastor who revealed that he had seen a picture of angels surrounding me and felt that God wanted me to know that I had his protection. At the time I thanked him for his words but didn't really receive them into my heart. It is only now that I can see how much I was protected that morning and in other mornings that followed. All too often I've looked at moments in my life and highlighted what went wrong, rather than highlighting what went right and how much protection I *did* receive.

One afternoon, some months later, I had just finished my paper round and was walking back to my house, ready to do a quick turnaround and head into town, when a friendly looking Pakistani man caught me with a hello outside the newsagents. He looked to be in his late twenties or early thirties, was quite attractive and had a friendly smile. Starting a conversation, he offered to drive me into the city centre to meet my friend as he was a taxi driver and heading that way anyway. I declined a couple of times but he firmly persuaded me to accept and ten minutes later I found myself sat in the passenger seat of his car.

A ten-minute car journey has never felt so long to me before or since as I gradually became aware of the vulnerable position I had placed myself in. My imagination began to run wild as it played with the idea that this man was completely in control now and I was very limited in my ability to stop anything negative from happening to me. Thankfully he stopped where I asked him to and I quickly made my departure, although not before he had given me a card and box of chocolates.

I hadn't met this man before and following this incident I made sure to avoid any further contact with him. During our car journey he told me how he had seen me several times before, whilst I had been out in the neighbourhood, and knew the times when I would be passing his house to deliver papers. The card he gave was full of flattery; the box of chocolates an attempt to seal my affections. Now, I can class his actions as the early stages of grooming a young person. At the time I was left with a chill down my spine as I knew, without any concrete proof, that I had just escaped a dangerous encounter.

Grooming is defined as the behaviours used by a predator to target and prepare a child or young person for sexual abuse or exploitation. They will often use very subtle methods that can be hard to detect, which most commonly involve taking on the role of a boyfriend and winning the victim's trust completely.

I will never really know what that guy's intentions were but I am thankful for the discernment that came into play during that car journey and prevented me from maintaining a relationship with him. There was certainly naivety on my part to get into the car with him in the first place, and it wasn't a wise decision, but I do believe I was protected by that which I cannot see.

In those first few years of living in Cobridge I realized that I had developed a fear of going outside. It wasn't the sort of fear that would prevent me from doing anything necessarily, but more that quiet sort of fear that whispers 'what ifs' into your ear and turns your imagination into a dark playground. Some of the experiences from my paper round confirmed these fears in me, and as not leaving the house wasn't an option, I learnt Psalm 23 off by heart and would whisper it on repeat as I walked through the streets.

> *The* Lord *is my shepherd, I lack nothing.*
> *He makes me lie down in green pastures,*
> *he leads me beside quiet waters,*
> *he refreshes my soul.*
> *He guides me along the right paths*
> *for his name's sake.*
> *Even though I walk*
> *through the darkest valley,*
> *I will fear no evil,*
> *for you are with me;*
> *your rod and your staff,*
> *they comfort me.*
>
> *You prepare a table before me*
> *in the presence of my enemies.*

You anoint my head with oil;
my cup overflows.
Surely your goodness and love will follow me
all the days of my life,
and I will dwell in the house of the LORD
for ever.
(Psalm 23)

Other instances occurred in those years, including one misty morning when a man jumped out of an alleyway and made a grab at me, pulling down his trousers in the process. I dodged him and bolted down the street, the sound of his eerie laughter following my beating heart. It was always my purity that attempts were made upon but, although I didn't leave Cobridge completely unscathed, Psalm 23 became my standard and testimony of protection.

There are many areas and places like Cobridge both in this country and the rest of the world, communities where the broken walk openly with their wounds and look for help in their simple greeting of 'hello'. They are places of exquisite beauty. By side-stepping those people who will probably bring a lot of inconveniences our way, we miss out on the pure joy of watching restoration, healing and love at work.

I would be lying if I said that I experienced this pure joy whilst I was living there. I think I carried more of a 'woe is me' attitude, but I consider it a privilege now to have called Cobridge home for five years. It was there that I learnt how to 'host the presence of God' long before I fully understood what that phrase meant, because in his presence there is no fear, no shame and no darkness, only purity, love and safety.

Pearls:

Zoe

I was sat in a pole-dancing bar in Thailand that appeared to only have trafficked women working there. Beneath the smiles and painted faces were beautiful pearls, each carrying their own heart-rending story. One woman in particular caught my attention and although I wasn't able to sit and hear her story, what I did learn of her has stayed with me and impacted my heart. She was from Russia and had been working in the bar for a few months as a dancer. It was clear as I watched her perform in the bar's 11 p.m. show that this woman wasn't just merely a good mover but she was a trained dancer. Her five-minute piece somehow miraculously managed to bring a touch of purity back into the room. Zoe's dance may actually be the most powerful piece that I've ever had the privilege of watching. She was dancing as if she was free.

Her choreography had been sexualized to appeal to her audience and fit the requirements of her bosses, but her heart was unveiled as she danced alone on the stage, her movements almost betraying her loneliness. I found tears welling up as I watched her and was reminded of members of my own family who have found their careers as performers on well-lit stages but have been saved from this backstreet darkness. I hated to see creativity that was intended to be displayed in purity, being so distorted and abused. Zoe wasn't made to dance on a stage in a strip bar, she was created in the image of God to display his glory and beauty.

Creativity releases life. It draws hope out of people's hearts and causes them to dare to dream again; it aids the restoration of a broken heart and enables eyes to see with fresh vision. When someone is denied access to the creativity that they were born with, and is instead given a distorted replica of the original, they are invited to witness the slow death of their hearts. The manner in which we steward creativity determines the health of the fruit we produce.

4

Reading Scars

Our bodies tell a story; every mark upon it speaks of a journey. Mine is lined in questions with arrows pointing to the pain of youth, the anger of misplaced identity and the marks of accidental injury. Camped out in the sun, my skin has soaked in its golden hues and given new shape to my story-riddled body. Every scar has been highlighted in pale white markers and I'm surprised afresh at the map of my journey that I carry.

You see, I used to hate my body, and my heart and mind were fuelled by angry questions: why was I alive? What use was I to the world? My body became a canvas for the outworking of hate and self-destruction as I began a regular rhythm of self-harming. My creativity was stunted in dark thoughts, angry images and a relentless hopelessness.

I remember one time trying to write a 'happy' poem and it's probably one of the worst things I've ever written. In frustration I screwed it up and threw it away, resigning myself to a future of depressing scribbles and morbid poetry.

I've never been one to shy away from the more uncomfortable topics in life and would much rather engage in a conversation about life and death than skirt awkwardly around the shallow waters of English weather. I remember being very concerned about the state of my classmates' souls at one point while I was in primary school, and made it my mission to check that they were all on good terms with God. I took each one aside during our breaks in the playground and asked whether or not they thought that they were going to heaven, certainly not a tactic I would choose to use now!

One memory that I hold clearly from my primary school years has a much darker content. Somehow I had grasped the concept of suicide and dramatically told one of my friends that I was going to kill myself that night. This of course did not happen and I turned up to school the next day, giving my poor friend some sort of excuse as to why I hadn't gone through with my threat. I had no intention of ending my life but, however large or small, there was a seed of desire within me to not be alive. This seed was forgotten about for a few years but grew to be unavoidable in my early teens.

In 2002, at the age of 13, the internet had been well and truly born and with it came the beginnings of social networking: instant messaging. I regularly logged into my MSN Messenger account to chat for several hours with my friends around the country and connect with those even further afield. I've always been a people person and I take great delight in meeting others with similar passions and desires. If you've ever been a member of a social networking site you'll know how common it is to have friend requests from complete strangers, who are often individuals that you'd rather avoid. As a woman in my twenties I now have no problem refusing those requests, but I didn't always show that same sense of self-protection, and became friends with a handful of people that I had never met face to face.

Jake told me he was 18, lived in America, was a Christian and had a girlfriend that he'd been dating for a while. I easily trusted him and we became friends. We would talk regularly and almost every time that I came online he would be there also. Our conversations soon became more personal and he was always interested as to whether I liked anyone or if anyone liked me. It became apparent that whether or not he had a girlfriend, he also wanted a relationship with me. I liked that he liked me and found myself wishing that he wasn't seeing anyone. I felt better about myself knowing that someone was interested in who I was.

It eventually transpired that Jake didn't have a girlfriend anymore and he soon became more vocal about his interests in me. So caught up was I in the desire to be found valuable and attractive to this man that I didn't refuse him when he asked me to visit certain websites and engage in sexual conversation. The feeling of being special and desired didn't last long and I soon began to feel dirty and ashamed, eventually dreading to see his name pop up in my chat window. I was scared to block him though and didn't dare tell anyone for fear of being labelled dirty and horrible. A friendship that had seemed so nice and safe had suddenly turned into something of completely the opposite nature. A little while later though, I blocked Jake from my contact list and never spoke to him again, burying the memory of this time until several years later.

In 2009 I was sat in an all-day training session on the effects of online paedophilia and internet safety. My colleague and I had begun drinking copious amounts of tea to fight against the afternoon drowsiness that had begun to creep up on us, encouraged by the free lunch and warm conference room. Our teacher of the day was unpacking the long-term effects caused by online sexual abuse and I found myself crashing into memories from my teens, my eyes open wide with revelation. Amongst the list of effects were 'low self-esteem, suicidal tendencies and self-harming behaviours.' I sat stunned as suddenly I connected the dots: The relationship that I had had with Jake had clearly abused the lines of trust and taken advantage of me both mentally and emotionally. As a result my self-esteem had dropped and I began to view my body as something with very little worth.

8 October 2004

Dear Hub,

Had a bad month really. Soon after the last time that I spoke to you, I started self-harming again. It's the worst it's ever been and maybe that's why I didn't speak to you for so long. All my insecurities came back, about the way that I look and stuff . . . then I exploded . . . I've never been so angry and it was all aimed at me. I hated myself so much. Anger and hatred consumed me . . . I felt all alone.

The seeds of depressive thinking that had been evident in my mind as a child had resurfaced with a vengeance around the time I was 13, particularly following my online encounters with Jake. I didn't like who I was one bit, I hated the body that I'd been forced to inhabit, and was angry at the God who had created me without asking my permission. I had many questions and disgruntled thoughts about life but my main one was, 'Why? Why am I alive? I never asked to be born so why did you create me, God? Why are all these things happening? Why do I have to feel such pain in my heart?'

Sometimes these questions could be heard like the quiet background noise of a TV on low volume. Other days they could be heard like a resounding gong, its vibrations affecting everything around it. However loud the volume though, I always listened to the voices.

By the time I was 14 or 15 I had developed a very well-established low self-esteem. I became an expert at comparing myself to others and constantly came out lacking, whether in character or physical appearance. I wanted to be affirmed and thought worthy of someone's affections yet at the same time held little love for myself.

When feelings of self-hatred are harboured in your heart, they can quite easily create a pool of anger that isn't hard to trigger, even by the smallest thing. I found this to be true of myself and would often feel a rage rising up within me that I learnt to become the target for. The anger did really stem from this root of self-hatred, and therefore it was very me-focused, but often others would get caught in the crossfire and I remember countless occasions when my siblings would be subjected to my explosions. It saddens my heart to remember those moments and how destructive 'seeing red' can be. Thankfully my family have never held it against me and have instead fiercely loved me through it all.

11 November 2004

So now I'm going through a withdrawal process concerning the self-harm. I haven't cut in nearly four days now. I never thought when I first cut that it would ever get so addictive or that it would be this painful to get out of.

My way of coping with negativity and events that caused me pain was to take it out on myself and I developed a pattern of self-harming. There were certain things that triggered it in me. A close friend of mine also struggled in this area and we would regularly confide in each other. My desire to help them was to the detriment of myself in the end and we had to say goodbye to our friendship. In an attempt to find others who understood and could help me, I also became a member of a couple of self-harm support websites where people could post their artwork, pictures and poems as well as talk to others in their chat room. Rather than help me get better however, these sites only opened my eyes to darker forms of self-harm and encouraged me to do more.

At the time I thought I would always be a self-harmer. I spoke to many people, some of whom were twice my age, and they all said the same thing: 'You never stop being a self-harmer.' Thankfully my life has proven them wrong and those statements turned out to be nothing more than lies.

13 March 2005

After football, I cut myself again . . . I'm not gonna do it again Hub. I realized just now that what my friend used to say to me was and is so true. Self-harming becomes so addictive . . . and each time, you hurt more people.

In the springtime of 2005 my family discovered what I'd been trying so hard to keep a secret. It was a moment that brought me a lot of shame as I uncovered my arms to reveal what my sleeves had been hiding, but in the long run it was the beginning of finding true freedom.

Many people get confused by the idea of self-harm; they don't understand it, and quite easily write the sufferer off as attention-seeking or following a trend. What a lot of people don't understand is that however it may start off for an individual, self-harming can become an addiction and a means by which they cope with situations or emotions that seem too overwhelming for them to handle. In my case I started to try to understand a close friend's pain and journey, who had been self-harming for longer than me and had begun to confide in me with their struggles. I wanted to help my friend and to be able to relate to the pain that they were feeling. A distorted idea began to form in my mind, and at the time made total sense, that if I wasn't here or if I cut myself more than they did, then they could have my happiness and they wouldn't need to hurt themselves anymore. It is that 'saviour' mentality that may seem quite noble to the thinker but is actually misplaced thinking. This developed into a way that I learnt to deal with my angry questions and release my pent-up emotions. At the time I didn't value my body so it actually seemed quite logical to take these things out on myself, rather than on people that I did love and value.

Once my secret had been uncovered by my parents, I began the lengthy process of getting well again and replacing my negative coping mechanisms with positive ones. This wasn't an overnight process for me and I would find myself relapsing from time to time. It was actually a few years before I finally felt free from the temptation to harm myself when things went wrong.

In September 2006 I moved back to Liverpool with my family and began being mentored by a lady in our church. Tamsin Evans became a pillar of love and support in my life and has continued to guide me, along with her husband, Nick. When she first took me under her wing, I was still very much struggling with negative thoughts and feelings towards myself. I wasn't self-harming but I hadn't really dealt with the issues that were at the root of it all. Over that following year and a half I went on quite an intense journey of changing the way that I think and embracing the truth about myself and this life.

I hit a set-back in all of this at the end of the summer of 2007. I wasn't finding it very easy to deal with some problems at home that my parents were facing. At the same time, I felt the relationship with my then boyfriend slowly slipping away, until it eventually came to an end in September. It suddenly seemed that everything was going wrong around me and I began to cope less and less well, coming to the conclusion that it was all my fault. I wanted out and made a feeble suicide attempt one night.

13 September 2007

> I think maybe I condemn myself a lot. I think I'm so in the mindset of failure and doing things wrong, that everything is automatically my fault.

It really is a horrible place to be in when it feels like there is no point in going on and the circumstances around you feel overwhelming. The situations that I was facing at that time might not seem that big an issue to some people, but to me they were tearing my heart apart. My vision had become one that looked too readily at the dark.

There is such a thing as loving people back to life though and I found my heart and mind becoming swiftly restored. In April of 2008 I took part in a women's weekend away that was organized by my church, Frontline. The weekend was full of teaching seminars, times of worship, and the opportunity to step out of the business of normal life and do a spiritual MOT. It was during these few days away in Wales that I finally understood the root cause of my self-harming and negative thinking. Once a root has been uncovered, a strategy can then be made to completely remove it so that the weed will never again return.

12 April 2008

The root of my depression, self-harm, and self-loathing is shame. Shame from all those moments that stick out in my memory where I got it wrong, both in public and in secret. Shame built upon shame which built upon shame until I was trapped and I didn't even realize it.

It's like my eyes have been opened to look back on different moments in my life and see another side to what happened. To own up where I got it wrong and to forgive and release where I felt wronged.

Shame has a lot to answer for and I believe it is something that we should be making war against. This is a trap that we've been falling into for years, since Adam and Eve walked in the garden and ate from the wrong tree, in fact. We've become masters at pointing out each other's faults rather than loving others out of their mistakes.

When someone is overcome by shame, they are bound by a painful feeling that is caused by something that they have done or by a dishonourable act that is done to them. It's almost a feeling that they are forced into and rather than helping them to make better choices in the future, it keeps them forever tied to that moment in their past. Guilt, however, is caused by the fact of doing wrong and allows them to take responsibility for their actions without being forever held to their moment of sin. Essentially when they find themselves covered in shame they no longer remember who they are and their vision becomes consumed by what they did wrong. Feelings of guilt, however, don't remove their identity but allow them to navigate through a process of restoration, forgiveness and releasing.

I do believe that we have created a habit of shaming people when they do things wrong, rather than establishing a culture of love and honour. I could point out a particular area of the world or a part of society that I think is worse in this than the others, but the truth is, it's a global issue.

If we were to choose honour instead of shame I do believe that we would see cases of suicide and self-harm plummet, that those who have been exploited would find their voice, and acts of injustice would decrease. I guess the problem with this idea is that we've just had too much fun in shaming people. Tabloids for example thrive on stories and images of celebrities, circled in bright red, where their bodies don't look perfect or they've been caught having an affair. We struggle to allow people to be free from that one thing that they did wrong and instead encourage a lifetime of striving to make up for past mistakes.

I was shown so much grace and honour by those around me, even when I may not have deserved it. On those darkest of days where I had given up hope and didn't believe that I could change, I had people spurring me on and loving me away from destruction.

As I spent more time worshipping God and focusing on him, I had fresh revelation of the price that Jesus paid for me when he died on the cross. I would punish myself because I thought that there was still a price to be paid; however, he has already paid that price in full.

Understanding the truth about what Jesus has done for me, and the victory over shame that he has won through sacrificing his life, has been like a key of freedom. The lies that I believed for years that I was worthless have been completely eradicated from my life and hold no place in my mind. I haven't self-harmed in years and I am rarely even tempted now. That which once took up so much of my time and thinking, has been completely defeated. I am not a self-harmer and I never will be again.

22 April 2008

I would be lying if I said that I'm feeling great joy now or am on some 'holy high'. I actually feel quite vulnerable and like something has been ripped from me. But I think those places that were filled with negativity have been broken. I know that they have.

God is going to fill those places with light, with peace and with vision for his kingdom instead of the kingdom of darkness.

'Forget the former things; do not dwell on the past. See, I am doing a new thing!' (Isaiah 43:18,19)

When something is burned it is destroyed forever, you cannot piece it back together. Even if you try to wear the ashes, they will just blow away.

5

Beauty for Ashes

Imagine creation in its purest form. Everything glows and shines with life and abundance. It's almost as if every fibre and atom is singing with joy, declaring their happiness and freedom to the rest of the world around them. Not one blade of grass is broken and the people you see from afar are clothed in garments that hold no blemish. A breeze lifts the hair from your shoulders and you breathe in deeply, suddenly aware of how content you are in this place, how much you want to make it home. The air is warm and everything just feels whole, complete, not lacking a thing. This is the scene that filled my mind as I stood with my eyes closed, listening to the swell of sweet worship around me. It was a warm day in the middle of May 2008 and I was on the first stop of a round-the-world trip. I had come to LA, a sprawling hub of creativity and beauty, to spend time with a boy that I barely knew at this point, but who was later to become my husband.

LA had been more of a last-minute addition to my trip but turned out to be the most significant place that I visited, both in terms of the people that I met and in the vision that was birthed within me. I was actually on my way to New Zealand to meet up with a childhood friend, who was finishing her gap year with Youth with a Mission (YWAM), before travelling to Australia together for a few weeks.

Months previously, before I had had a chance to book my flights, I received a phone call one night whilst I was hanging out with some friends back in the UK. 'Hey Joy, remember me? It's Phillip!' I was stood in my friend's hallway feeling slightly giddy as I'd just been eating pink fairy cakes that were generously covered in glitter and filled with sugar, but I definitely remembered him. Phillip's home was in LA, but he had been visiting the UK when we'd met about a year and a half beforehand, whilst I was working for Youth for Christ (YFC) in Stoke-on-Trent for my gap year. 'Hi Phillip! Yes I remember you, how are you doing?' 'Doing great! I'm with Mark and we're just driving down to Stoke now from Edinburgh. We're actually near Preston now, can we come and see you?' Mark was a good friend of mine that I had worked with at YFC and had first introduced me to Phillip. It turned out that Phillip had come to the UK to celebrate the New Year in Edinburgh and to visit friends of his both up in Scotland and in England. 'You'd like to come to Liverpool . . . now?' 'Yeah, we'll be with you in about an hour!' 'Um . . . sure! I'm at my friend's house but you're more than welcome to come by.' 'Great! We'll see you soon!' I hung up and stared at my phone, slightly amazed, before the giddy feeling returned and I went back into the lounge to announce the newcomers.

It was around midnight when the boys arrived, just as it had begun to snow and the streets of Wavertree, Liverpool took on a quiet, magical air. It could have been the fact that I had just watched *Enchanted* earlier that evening, but I felt there was something significant about that night as we all sat around till the early hours of the morning, before the boys finally left to carry on their journey to Stoke and I made my own way home.

Over the following two weeks I couldn't stop thinking about that random, magical evening when this American boy, with a smile that lights up any room, had appeared with Mark for no other reason than to see me. I've since discovered that strategy is one of my strengths, which came into play when I found myself deciding that I could 'drop in' to LA on my way to New Zealand later that year. I suggested this via email to an unsuspecting Phillip and soon LA was added to my itinerary.

Fast forward again to May 2008 when my visit with Phillip led me to find myself in a cute apartment with a group of welcoming and passionate men and women that now called LA home, as we prayed for the ending of human trafficking. The meeting was being led by a lady in Phillip's church who was also the director in LA of NightLight, a not-for-profit organization that works with women who have been trafficked in LA and Bangkok. It was this organization that I later ended up working with in 2012 when I visited Thailand.

Human trafficking wasn't a phrase that I had really become acquainted with before. I knew lots about prostitution, sexual abuse and the porn industry but trafficking was an area of exploitation that was new to me. I felt my heart become broken and captivated to fight this issue of injustice and my eyes were opened to see people that I didn't know still existed: slaves.

The recruitment, transportation, transfer, harbouring or receipt of persons, by means of the threat or use of force or other forms of coercion, of abduction, of fraud, of deception, of the abuse of

power or of a position of vulnerability or of the giving or receiving
of payments or benefits to achieve the consent of a person having
control over another person, for the purpose of exploitation.[1]

In many ways there is a lot about human trafficking that we
do not know. It is a secretive, black market trade that operates
under the covers of darkness and deception. However, chinks
have been made in its armour and more is being understood
about it every day.

- It is estimated that 2.5 million people are in forced labour
  (including sexual exploitation) at any given moment as a
  result of trafficking.
- 161 countries are reported to be either a source, transit or
  destination country for human trafficking.
- The majority of victims are between 18 and 24 years old,
  95% of them experiencing physical or sexual violence
  during their time of forced labour.
- It is estimated that 1.2 million children are trafficked
  each year.[2]

More and more people are being mobilized all over the world
to stand up and combat this horrendous world trade, making
it their aim to raise awareness, bring perpetrators to justice,
rescue those in bondage and campaign to the law makers for
their support. The task of seeking justice and freedom is a
huge one but not impossible.

William Wilberforce is one of my heroes when I start thinking of the enormity of this idea of ending human trafficking.
He gave his life to fighting for justice and a change in laws

that would bring about freedom for many in captivity. There was only one of him but already there are many of us who are making a stand against this injustice and demanding that it stop. Therefore it must be possible.

The scene of pure creation filled my mind as we prayed together that evening in LA and one of the women sang out. I don't remember what the words were that she uttered, or if they were even in English, but in that moment my spirit responded and I found myself watching a scene play out as if it were a clip from a movie; creation in its purest form.

Walking through this perfect scenery were women dressed in grey cloaks, covered in dust, their shoulders stooped. Suddenly a wind swept across the land, not violently but with a gentle power, blowing the cloaks away and revealing a new attire, glowing white robes that spoke only of glory and power, immediately causing you to forget the shadows in which you had just seen them draped. The whole countenance of these women changed and they became who they were clearly always meant to be: beautiful. As I watched them continue on their way a Scripture came to mind that I realized was an exact description of what I had just seen:

> *The Spirit of the Sovereign LORD is on me,*
> *because the LORD has anointed me . . .*
> *. . . to bestow on them a crown of beauty*
> *instead of ashes,*
> *the oil of joy*
> *instead of mourning,*
> *and a garment of praise*
> *instead of a spirit of despair.*

They will be called oaks of righteousness,
a planting of the LORD
for the display of his splendour.
(Isaiah 61:1–3)

Beauty for ashes. This was a promise. A promise that is for them, for the broken, for the enslaved, for those that feel like all they have to offer is ashes. Words that were spoken out and written down by an old prophet were ringing true again in my ears, thousands of years later. Hope was rising in my heart and with it a belief that things could change, and that we could change it.

My time in LA came to a close and I boarded a flight to New Zealand to carry on with my travels, already having experienced so much change in my heart and the vision that I held for my future. The weeks that followed continued to build on what had already been started in me as I began to learn more about the international slave trade of human trafficking. Slavery was meant to have been abolished in 1833 thanks to the hard work of Wilberforce who earnestly petitioned for freedom in the United Kingdom, but here I was in 2008 discovering that slavery was as alive and well as ever and in a potentially much more sinister form. I felt the weight of this new information but at the same time the encouragement of the promise that God will restore 'beauty instead of ashes'. Something was being birthed within me: a desire to not let Wilberforce's work to have been in vain but to continue to see all forms of slavery abolished.

You may choose to look the other way but you can never say again that you did not know.

William Wilberforce

These words have stuck with me over the last few years as I've let my heart and mind be opened further to what is occurring all over this world, and have encouraged me to not stop talking about it. I don't want to choose to look the other way. I want to be able to keep looking straight ahead even if my vision becomes filled with another person's pain and suffering. By allowing myself to see, I am then in a position to act and by acting, I am one more thorn in the enemy's side.

From this point on, human trafficking became a regular part of my vocabulary and would often find its way into conversations. In my workplace, at a city-centre tea shop and bar, some of my regular customers affectionately nicknamed me 'the human trafficker' just because I was constantly talking about it!

In August 2008, just a month and a half after returning from my travels, I joined the Liverpool base of Pure Creative Arts (Pure), a registered charity that works with young people across the UK with a vision of seeing them realize and be released into their full potential. It was during those first few weeks of working there that I took some time out one afternoon in the prayer room that we had in our office, to ask God for fresh vision for my future and the areas that I was passionate about. I clearly remember being stood in the room, the warm sunlight soaking everything in its glory, music gently playing in the background, and I was reminded of the vision that I had had in LA of creation in its purest form. Then a new image began filling my mind. I saw a white mansion with rooms that were filled with creativity – music, design, dance, art – and in every room were women. Women who had once been broken, who had had their creativity distorted in the name of exploitation and were now finding restoration. They were finding hope and were being given a new life. My heart became alive as I began to dream afresh and the idea of Beauty for Ashes was formed.

My dream is to see houses of restoration all around the world for women who are coming out of the sex industry where they can live in safety and love. They will be places where women can have their creativity and purity restored, not forever tied to the traumas that they have experienced but finding freedom and wholeness, however long that journey may take them.

4 December 2008

This is now my vision for what God wants me to dedicate my life to.

The women in that vision are the ones that God wants me to find, work with, and help restore.

I began to see creativity restored. Where it had been used as a weapon against women, where it had been stolen and held captive, I saw it bring healing. I saw it bring release and restoration.

I began to get a vision of a school. A school of creativity and restoration. Women came to this school who had previously been trafficked, exploited, been robbed of everything that they are entitled to as a human being. In this school they began to find release, they began to dream again for the first time and out of the restoration of creativity came the restoration of self. Whole again.

> *I see women with cloaks of ashes being washed and given a new*
> *wardrobe,*
> *Beautiful white robes of purity that shine,*
> *That glorify their Father and Creator.*
> *They are women warriors.*
> *They are not afraid to fight or fearful of war.*
> *Their hearts burn, an all-consuming flame of passion right to*
> *their core.*
> *And their mandate is freedom.*
> *Their testimony is victory.*
> *Their banner is joy.*
> *They walk through mountain tops and sing creation's song.*

> *Let justice reign!*

I still hold this dream in my heart, a treasure that rests there wrapped in hope, waiting to be fulfilled. I believe that God birthed this dream within me at the time that he did, to spur me on and ready myself for when the time is right for Beauty for Ashes to start. This vision then became the fuel that has sent me all over the world, meeting many extraordinary people and opening my eyes to the reality of modern-day slavery. I don't want to be a naive white woman who starts something with no real idea of what she's doing: I want to be as equipped as I can be with a foundation of prayer and a history with God that can declare his faithfulness and victory even in the hardest of circumstances.

Pearls:

Louise

There's one pearl that I met several years ago who will always be a precious woman to me. I guess you could say that we met by accident, but for anyone who believes in divine appointments, I would have to take your side. I was at a Christian event that friends of mine were running in the Midlands when I was asked to pray for some people who had been impacted by the evening, and wanted someone to stand with them and minister to them. I hadn't met Louise before but approached her with a smile and asked if there was anything that I could pray for her. We ended up sat on one side of the room talking and praying together well after the meeting had come to a close.

Louise had grown up in England in a well-respected family that went to church every week and raised her as a young woman with a firm faith in God. At the age of 11 she began being violently sexually abused by a family friend and, on occasions, some of his friends. Her parents were unaware of the trauma that she was experiencing on a regular basis and her trust in men quickly began to disintegrate and disappear. She fell pregnant as a teenager and, although she wanted to love and cherish the new life in her womb, she ended up having an abortion in response to the fear and loneliness that she felt. Desiring intimacy but hating men, Louise began seeing women and by the time she was in university was leading a fully fledged homosexual lifestyle. Although her physical and emotional needs were being met, there were deep wounds beneath the surface and a pattern of people controlling and manipulating her could clearly be seen. As a result of all that Louise had been through, she was struggling with patterns of self-harming and disordered eating when I met her. The cry of her heart as I began talking with her was for things to change but hope had become a faint possibility rather than a present reality.

We prayed together that night but the real changes came over the years that followed as we met up for coffee or when she would come to visit me in Liverpool for a few days at a time. As I watched I began to see this woman change from a quiet, fearful girl who hid behind her insecurities to a woman who is now fully pursuing her dreams and living out of a whole heart. I've watched her take brave step after step as she's faced up to the horrendous things of her past and allowed healing to enter in and restore her childhood. She chose to end a relationship with a woman that had her bound by control and is now in a place where she desires to be with a man again. The flashbacks have got less intense and don't cripple her heart for days like they used to. She knows what her true identity is and has her gaze fixed firmly on the prize, to rest in Daddy's arms.

Louise's journey has been long, and she's still travelling on it now, but it inspires me on those days when I question what the point of it all is. Sometimes a prayer can seem so small and insignificant when compared with the scale of the atrocities that we hear about and see, but those words we utter travel further than we know and carry the power to demolish mountains. My friendship with Louise started with a prayer and it has continued that way as we keep in touch from around the world. I am so proud of this woman and view it as such a privilege to have witnessed the restoration in her life.

Restoration isn't an overnight job. It doesn't work like painkillers that you take before you go to bed to get rid of a headache, but it is an investment of patience, love and time. Those of us who dare to take up the challenge to love the one in front of us, brokenness and all, get welcomed into a journey that can be messy and painful but is nevertheless glorious. Seeing lives restored involves removing the pile of ashes that their cut-up hands are holding and replacing it with beauty. The beauty of freedom and truth, hope and love, a renewed vision and the courage to dare to love again. Restoring the past takes time but the end result far exceeds what they started with as each individual begins to stand unimpaired by their brokenness. The cracks that used to appear so starkly to them then become filled with gold, creating beauty that far exceeds anything that they have previously carried.

I have had many people agree to take up the challenge to love me through to complete restoration and my life hasn't remained the same as a result. There have been times when it would have felt easier to let my brokenness win, but no matter how loud the voice of our past might be, the roar of an impassioned restorer is far more ferocious.

6

Loving Mercy & Walking Humbly

8 November 2008

I went to The Stand in Birmingham, an event to cause the church to rise up and come against the issue of human trafficking and slavery in our nation and world. It was 8 hours of back-to-back bands and speakers, times of prayer and worship, all with a passion to see an end to human abuse and slavery. For me it was a time to be re-envisioned for the call that God has on my life: that I am here to fight for justice. That something great can be accomplished through me, in my lifetime. Greater things are yet to come, greater things are still to be done.

It's very easy to go to meetings, to watch a powerful documentary, to hear someone's story and be really moved in the moment. It's much harder to take that moment and do something with it; it's much harder to act. I get moved all of the time, sometimes I don't even know why; I'll just watch someone walk by and the sight of their slightly stooped shoulders or the gait of loneliness that they carry touches my heart, and I know that there goes someone in dire need of a hug. I don't go around hugging people though, in fact most of the time I don't do anything but ask God to bless them and carry on walking. I find it a challenge to know when to act when my eyes are opened to see so many people in differing places of need. Maybe I should start hugging everyone but I feel that might get me in more trouble than actually helping anybody!

After going to The Stand event with a group of people from my church, Frontline, in Liverpool, I got involved in one of many Active Communities against Trafficking (ACT groups) that were starting across the country. Stop the Traffik is a global movement of individuals, communities and organizations fighting to prevent human trafficking around the world and our Liverpool community began working in conjunction with them, led by a friend of mine, Brenda Garner.

I am definitely someone who likes to take action on things that I'm passionate about: once I've made my mind up about something I'm all in and want to get going straight away. Therefore being a part of a group called ACT was a perfect beginning for me to start doing something to combat this issue of trafficking. The group meets regularly in Liverpool to share with each other where they are up to, giving any fresh ideas and encouraging each other to make our city a slave-free zone.

Over the last few years the Liverpool ACT group has been responsible for putting on different awareness-raising events in the city and starting both national and international campaigns to help prevent trafficking. It's been amazing to be a part of such a diverse group of people who have all come together to fight for justice.

In November 2009 I co-ordinated an event at the International Slavery Museum in Liverpool, for city leaders and church members alike to again raise awareness in the city. For months running up to the evening I worked with a group of local performers to produce a piece on human trafficking that was then used for the evening and Ben Cooley, CEO of Hope for Justice, came and spoke. Nothing particularly life-changing happened that night, in fact it revealed gaps in our knowledge and pointed towards what we needed to work on next, but it gathered people together and provided an opportunity to speak truth.

Then in early 2010 I was getting a cab back home late one night from a friend's house. My driver immediately engaged me in conversation as we pulled out of the side street and back onto the main road home. He had just dropped some young girls into town and began grumbling about their age and the things he had to see in his job. I was intrigued:

'So what exactly do you see in your job?'

'Oh everything, babe, I know where all the drug houses and the brothels are. I've had all sorts of people sit in my car and I just have to look the other way, know what I mean?'

'Yeah . . .' My mind was racing with things that I wanted to say, questions I had and also a desire to ask him to show me where everything was. I began talking to him about trafficking, asking if he ever saw anything that looked like people were being exploited. He told me that he had and described a couple of occasions to me. We were nearly at my house now so I decided to go for gold.

'Would you ever be interested in helping out with the ACT group that I'm a part of?'

'Ah no love, I've got enough on my plate, know what I mean? If you had a number for us to call though when we see something, I can do that. I just can't get involved in no charity work.'

'Sure, thanks anyway, it's been great chatting to you.'

I left the car and made my way inside. It was about 3 a.m. but I was completely awake now. We needed to target the taxis. We needed the taxi drivers on board.

Following my late night conversation I spoke to Brenda at the ACT group and we formed a plan to start a campaign that would send information out to all of the taxi drivers in the city about what trafficking was and how they could help combat it. This taxi campaign became national earlier this year with the Home Office encouraging cities across the UK to use it. Fourteen local authorities in England are now using the campaign stickers or posters and are running events with cabbies. Other ACT groups are now running the campaign in the UK; one group had an article in one of the biggest taxi magazines, and another has an invitation to present at the national forum for taxi drivers. The campaign is also being replicated in Northern Ireland, Scotland, Gambia and India. It amazes me how big an impact one conversation has gone on to have! I am now no longer able to have much involvement with the Liverpool group but they are continuing to build successful campaigns and doing great preventative work in the city.

When I first found out about human trafficking, I made a decision in my heart and mind that I needed to act. There were so many questions that I had about it and so many things I wanted to get better at and to have experience in. Since that time in 2008 I've put myself in training, going to places that would teach me more about these areas of sexual exploitation and offering my time to practically work with those in need on my doorstep.

Streetwise is a project that aims to practically serve street sex workers in Liverpool, to provide emotional and spiritual support, and to link them with appropriate services. In 2009 I joined the many volunteers recruited by Streetwise to go out on a Friday and Saturday night to the red-light district in Liverpool's city centre. Each team consists of about four people with a simple mission of loving well. The teams go out in a van that is loaded with hot drinks, sandwiches and condoms to be given out to the girls and provides somewhere for them to come and sit and talk, away from the often chilly night air. Last year Streetwise had around 829 visits to the van, giving out 1,262 condoms and providing 1,156 hot drinks. It has become a lifeline to many of the women.

Sophia has been on the streets for a long time now. Growing up in a household where she was regularly abused both physically and sexually, it wasn't long before she found herself being exploited by others. She became addicted to alcohol and drugs during her teens and, although she's had periods of sobriety since then, they have remained a part of her lifestyle. I came into contact with Sophia soon after I started volunteering for Streetwise. As one of the older working women and louder characters, she was known by everyone.

In an environment where sex work and addiction walk hand in hand, you can often find a web of lies surrounding each fragile heart in an attempt to mask the shame and pain that is often hidden there. Unfortunately this is something that has been very evident in working with Sophia and we have often had to pick between what is truth and what is lies. Aside from the difficulties though I have found it a real honour to be able to draw alongside Sophia.

In 2010 she fell pregnant with a baby boy and although there were a couple of scares along the way he was born healthy and without any trouble. Unfortunately, due to the unstable lifestyle that Sophia was living, he was immediately taken into foster care and later adopted. However, in the time in-between, I had the privilege of seeing Sophia in a completely different role. She wasn't a sex worker as she stood in the hospital ward holding this precious little life: she was a mother.

Sophia is still working in the red-light district and although she has had many offers of help, she hasn't been able to conquer her addictions and is still accessing the support of Streetwise. I would much rather be able to tell a story that speaks of having seen freedom but I share this journey as one that isn't finished but rather is one where we continue to choose to love regardless of its ups and downs. This choice doesn't spell out a walk in the park, and is often far from easy, but love is the greatest commandment that we, as followers of Christ, have been given and therefore the one that we at Streetwise have chosen to follow.

Jesus replied: "'Love the Lord your God with all your heart and with all your soul and with all your mind." This is the first and greatest commandment. And the second is like it: "Love your neighbour as yourself."'
(Matthew 22:37–39)

In all of the women that I've had the immense privilege of working with or meeting for a brief moment, such as through Streetwise, I have seen huge potential for greatness. Maybe for many people who pass by women who work in the sex industry they see someone who is of lesser value than them, maybe they don't even give them a second thought, or maybe their thoughts are all of judgement. We don't often view people who are clearly broken, in need and selling themselves as having potential. However, when you take the time to stop, when you pause from your routine and sit with them, when you look into their eyes and call them by their real name, not their working one, you begin to unearth the greatness that they were created for; you begin to glimpse the gold within them.

'It's been such a horrible day, so horrible, I just don't understand why she did it!' I was sat in the back of the Streetwise van on a cold Friday night opposite a woman who was relaying her painful accounts of the day. That morning she'd been arrested on false charges of domestic violence that her girlfriend had made towards her. She'd spent the whole day in a cell, being interviewed by people who automatically made judgements of her because of her occupation, before her girlfriend finally dropped the charges and she was released. She cried as she said how ashamed she'd felt as the police officers searched her and made her get undressed in front of them.

As I listened my heart broke for her. I knew some of what she was feeling, some of the shame that was wrapping itself around her heart. Earlier that year I had been arrested after I walked through the wrong door in a subway station in New York. I didn't understand the charges that were brought against me and found myself caught in a moment of injustice. In that moment of standing handcuffed and being walked to the police station I had had to make a conscious effort not to bow down to shame. Now I found myself in a position to use my own experiences to relate better to a woman who may see her life far removed from mine. She didn't have a circle of support like I have and didn't have a belief system as her foundation that taught her that she's worthy of love, respect and honour. Instead she had a lifetime of people telling her that she was worthless, no one calling her beautiful but instead treating her body like an object. Her day's accounts only reaffirmed those beliefs to her precious heart.

I held her hands and carried on listening as she poured out her heart and her story. Straight away I loved her completely. It's often so easy to make judgements of people or to assume that because we see them doing one act, having an addiction or making poor choices that therefore their whole life is a write-off. Something tells me though that that's not meant to be our response.

After a while of listening I asked if I could pray for her, something that I've found to be the most helpful first act in loving someone. She consented and as I held her hands I reaffirmed her beauty and worth before God, asking that he bring comfort and help to her precious heart. With tears running down her cheeks she shared how that was the most beautiful thing anyone had said about her in years.

After leaving the van to work, she later returned to sit for a bit as she was afraid of some of the men who were walking around the area. I saw the fear in her eyes then and the tiredness that she carried from living a life that doesn't allow you to relax but keeps you alert for your own safety.

'There is no way that anyone can enjoy this life,' were the words that she later uttered to me. This lady's story broke my heart and also brought fresh value to my own journey as I realized that some of my own trials are not to be walked through in vain. Good really can come from those experiences that we find the hardest if we share them through the voice of love. Sometimes loving people is the simplest thing and all it requires of us is to hold their hands and tell them that they're beautiful when no one else will.

I love to hear the dreams that the women have, from the big picture stuff to the little day-to-day things that they would love to have or be able to do. There have been moments of being sat in the back of the Streetwise van, everyone enjoying a hot cup of tea when I think for a second it's been forgotten what we're all doing there, as suddenly the place is alive with dreams and the small, simple hopes of their hearts have been voiced and heard.

When we open our eyes and allow ourselves to look beyond the physical evidence before us, we can begin to see the stunning beauty of who we really are. I think in some ways God asks us all to be 'International Treasure Hunters': to be people who naturally look for the hidden jewels within those that we meet. Sometimes calling attention to that treasure can mean telling someone how stunning they are, that they are not worthless but they are completely lovable. Other times it can look like identifying a skill or quality in someone that they do not believe they have, and encouraging them to run with a dream that they didn't think was worth letting become a reality.

I am surrounded by many who make it a normal part of their lives to call out the gold in those around them. There have been countless occasions when people have chosen to encourage and spur me on by telling me what I could not see myself. Many times I've teetered on the edge of giving up or have believed in a lie for a while and someone has stopped, looked me in the eyes and lovingly brought truth to me that has helped me take a deep breath and carry on. If I need that, as someone who has been brought up in a loving and safe family where my needs have been provided for, how much more does the person need it whose family rejected them and they've been the receiver of years of abuse and lies?

9 December 2008

I pray that when I look at people I would see Jesus in them. I pray that I would then tell them what I see.
Amen.

I remember praying this prayer, stood at a night of worship, and it has become a standard that I've tried to uphold ever since. We were all created in the image of God, therefore we all have elements of him in us no matter what our occupation may be or even what our belief systems are. God is within each of us but sometimes we just need someone to point him out to us.

My journals are littered with scraps of paper, Post-it notes and cards that people have given to me over the years where they've taken the time to write down words of encouragement to me. Some of those messages have spoken into my future and the dreams that I hold in my heart, some were very timely for that particular moment and some are words that I return to time and time again as they remind me of who I am.

One of the cards that I have stuck in a more recent journal was given to me by one of the women that I have come to know through Streetwise. The words that she wrote always humble me every time that I read them as they simply thank me for being there and encouraging her on a day when she had given up hope. On my part it didn't seem like I had done any great feat, but for her to hear words of truth at that point had saved her and brought her life.

What can I say, you brought me out of a very dark place and I genuinely believe that because of your love talking to me on the phone, and your prayer, that you saved my life. I was so confused and depressed. I feel so much better and I know in my heart that Jesus loves me. Thank you.

There is such power in what we speak out over ourselves and those around us. One of the proverbs puts this best:

The tongue has the power of life and death, and those who love it will eat its fruit.
(Proverbs 18:21)

I love life! I love to declare goodness and truth over people and see life literally return to their countenance. This is the gift that we daily walk with and yet so often misuse; we have the opportunity to bring life to those we encounter. What we choose to speak out informs the atmosphere around us and has the potential to love people back to life.

Of course the wrong choice of words can also be very destructive, whether they are aimed at ourselves as we look in the mirror or spoken out in a moment of anger or frustration. There are countless times when I know that I have spoken out death, either over myself or to someone else, and have wished that I could just take the words back as I witnessed the damage that they caused. I'm so glad that such a thing as grace and forgiveness exists!

In choosing to answer the command that God gave us 'To act justly and to love mercy' (Micah 6:8), we may not always have the time to sit down with a person and have an in-depth conversation about the Bible, who God is and what Jesus has done for us, but we will always have the opportunity to show love. That can be as simple as looking at someone in the eyes when everyone else looks at their body, or telling someone that their life is beautiful and precious: we don't need to complicate love.

> *Love is patient, love is kind. It does not envy, it does not boast,*
> *it is not proud. It does not dishonour others, it is not self-*
> *seeking, it is not easily angered, it keeps no record of wrongs.*
> *Love does not delight in evil but rejoices with the truth. It*
> *always protects, always trusts, always hopes, always perseveres.*
> *(1 Corinthians 13:4–7)*

7

Hold on to Hope

I've often wished that my life could play out like a musical, where you don't have to say anything but the music starts playing and the audience immediately knows what you're thinking and feeling. Words can sometimes seem to lack the depth that I need in order to express what a moment meant to me or how a situation unfolded. I think for this part of my story I would prefer for a musical interlude, but we can't always have what we want, so I shall just have to do my best with words.

The year 2009 had a very exciting and romantic start as I welcomed in the New Year in New York with Phillip. It was at this point that we decided to pursue a relationship together and, whilst sat on the floor in Borders by Columbus Circle, he officially became my boyfriend. After a week of being together he then flew back to LA and I made what ended up being a long journey home to Liverpool with my sister and a friend. The three of us became stuck in JFK airport for twenty-four hours as flight after flight was overbooked and we were finally squeezed on a plane home, all thoroughly ready to leave New York.

As I sat in the airport with my journal, I wrote out Psalm 139 as a declaration over myself and the year ahead and to still the voices that whispered I wasn't worth the potential that I could see before me.

You have searched me, LORD,
and you know me.
You know when I sit and when I rise;
you perceive my thoughts from afar.
You discern my going out and my lying down;
you are familiar with all my ways.
Before a word is on my tongue
you, LORD, know it completely.
You hem me in behind and before,
and you lay your hand upon me.
Such knowledge is too wonderful for me,
too lofty for me to attain.

Where can I go from your Spirit?
Where can I flee from your presence?
If I go up to the heavens, you are there;
if I make my bed in the depths, you are there.
If I rise on the wings of the dawn,
if I settle on the far side of the sea,
even there your hand will guide me,
your right hand will hold me fast.
(Psalm 139:1–10)

Upon returning home to Liverpool I resumed my schedule of working on a voluntary basis for Pure and part-time for Leaf, a tea shop based in Liverpool city centre. I suddenly became a regular attendee on Skype and obsessed with checking my emails as I began navigating how to be in a long-distance relationship. I soon discovered that it wasn't as easy a journey as my dreamy head had hoped but quickly became used to having to handle different time zones and the insecurities that surfaced due to distance.

Anyone that has had the experience of being separated from their loved one by many miles and long periods of time will tell you the importance of communication, understanding the other's needs and how to meet them when you can't be physically present. Comfort is not found so easily when a hug is not available to ease an aching heart and instead a source that is greater than our mortal selves has to be found. I found that source of comfort to be God. In those early months of 2009 I battled with the insecurities of not feeling worthy of this new relationship and the fear that it would end. Being someone who has been blessed with a very active imagination, it didn't take long for my anxious mind to convince me of things that weren't true.

Although these thoughts and anxieties were very real at the time, upon looking back through my journals the resounding experience was one of love and encounters with God, the source of all love who encouraged me, strengthened me and spoke truth to a heart that was asking to be held with care. Unless we are connected to the Source it is quite easy for the love that we have to run dry and peter out, causing relationships to suffer. I learnt during this season just where my confidence needed to come from and where to look for my security; it wasn't to a man but it was to my Father, *Abba* Father.

30 January 2009

I've been taken on a love encounter, a journey deeper into the heart of God. All the love that I have comes from him, he is the Source. And this love keeps growing; it is like my heart has been expanded. I've been dipped in the honey; I've tasted the sweetness of his presence; I've begun wading deeper into his river . . . and it's glorious!

At the beginning of April my relationship with Phillip came to a sudden end during a visit that he made to the UK and I found myself completely floored, unable to comprehend why this had happened. I later learnt that Phillip had felt that it wasn't the right time for us to be together and for us to really grow as a couple we needed to be able to live in the same city rather than negotiating our relationship over thousands of miles. At that time, Phillip was also going through a hard time with his family and they needed to be a higher priority than a long-distance relationship.

As the reality of the break-up began to sink in I tried desperately to cling on to the promises and words of encouragement that I had been hearing so clearly in the previous few months, whilst fighting the temptations of old coping mechanisms that were throwing themselves back in my face. It was in this time that I needed to maintain a strong connection with the Source of all love that I had been leaning into in the months running up to this point, a task that can often be easier said than done when suddenly love doesn't seem that trustworthy a force.

My initial response was to go into self-protection mode, denying that anything was wrong and refusing to tell anyone, because once you voice something it becomes a reality and when something is real it can't be taken back. I managed this for about two days and sat through a friend's wedding without dropping a tear, before I finally let the mask fall and allowed my heart to break. Once broken we are then in the perfect position to be put back together again.

6 April 2009

I'm tired and broken. I'm tired of living in this body that seems to fall into pain far too easily. I'm tired of being the one that gets broken.

But I'm learning that it's okay to be broken, it's okay to hurt as long as you let God into that pain, you let him own it. He has given me the strength to stand in this time so I need to take hold of it and push through.

He is never going to leave me. He's always going to hold me because he is my father and he loves me. His love is not ordinary, reserved for a certain time or season, but it goes on. It never stops pursuing me, running over me, loving me.

We can often mistake our brokenness for weakness, believing the lie that because we are not singing about rainbows and butterflies but would much rather be rocking and crying in a corner, that there is something deeply wrong with us. That's not altogether true: in those moments we are merely showing our humanity and displaying the need for a comforter and healer, someone who is greater than our pain and distress.

I do believe that we need to get better at creating a culture where brokenness doesn't bring shame and our answer isn't to just supply bandages, but our solution every time is to take them to God the Healer.

As I stumbled through my own brokenness I tried my best to remember this truth and think upon those noble, right, pure and lovely things, but all too soon I began to give in to the offers of quick-fix help and short term comforts. A tendency of mine during difficult seasons is to throw myself into work and fill up my diary so that alone time is minimized and space to think is removed. It didn't take long before I was working day and night shifts back to back between two jobs, creating plenty of barriers in my heart from having to feel anything and therefore deal with anything. Within a month I had successfully created an environment where I could operate and do what needed to be done but had become completely emotionally numb.

On 23 May I suddenly realized the dangerous place that I had let myself come to, and what had begun with a broken heart had now spiralled into my becoming a woman without hope or any care for herself or her future. It may seem like a very overly dramatic place to have come to, simply after having experienced a relationship break-down, but I believe that similar stories happen all the time simply because we neglect to look after our hearts properly and instead choose options that numb the pain rather than properly processing it.

That Saturday morning I felt a warning in my spirit to be careful as I realized in a short moment of revelation that I had lost all awareness for my own safety. I instead chose to ignore that still, small voice and continue on in my pattern of hard-heartedness, deciding that I didn't care anyway. It's a moment that I look back on with sadness, choosing not to regret it, but wishing that I had listened.

A night out had been organized by my friends and I joined them that evening, drinking from the start and spending a lot of time with a group of lads that I had met earlier in the week who were visiting Liverpool. Before long I was pretty drunk and had the sole attention of one of the guys that we were with. It wasn't until the following morning, when I was piecing the night back together and had a string of text messages in my inbox asking if I was okay, that I realized how vulnerable I had let myself become. Unfortunately it was a realization that came a little too late as I awoke to the stark evidence that my virginity, that I had been so careful to protect, had been taken from me.

The guy that I'd been with offered to take me home and, knowing I was ready for bed, I happily agreed. I'd never let someone that I barely knew take me home before but I really didn't think much of it and remember offering to make him a cup of tea as we made our way through the front door. It was a bank holiday weekend so neither of my house-mates were at home and I kicked off my painful shoes in the hallway, welcoming the cool touch of the wooden floor to my tired soles. I then began giving my companion a tour of the house, gripping the staircase to steady myself as we made our way upstairs. I don't know why I thought he needed a tour but maybe somewhere underneath my drunken haze was a discomfort with this strange man being in my home.

My memory doesn't serve me too well on the details of how things progressed from there but before I knew it we were in my bedroom and he was in my bed. For a split second it was like I suddenly sobered up and my brain caught up with everything that was happening. I didn't want to be here like this, I didn't want to have sex with him: I wanted to get out. 'Wait. I've not done this before and . . .' I tried to get the words out that I wanted to communicate. 'Shhhhh!' He stopped me mid-flow and in that moment it was like a cloud enveloped me and I sank back into it, away from what was happening to my body. Just like when I was a teenager and I would create whole other worlds in my head to escape into as I walked the streets of Cobridge, I tried to romanticize that night and make it seem okay. I tried to ignore the voices that told me that it was wrong, that it shouldn't have been like that and that he should have listened to me. I tried to ignore the flashbacks that began to torture my mind and make me relive those moments that I was trying so hard to forget.

24 May 2009

I'm tainted now, damaged goods forever. No wonder all of the good guys dump me. I'm trouble. All I do is ruin things.

It's the morning after and I'm lying in my bed with the morning sunshine soaking me. He is asleep next to me, one arm wrapped around my bare body. My mouth is dry and I feel sick. I want to get out of bed. I want a shower. I want to be clean, but I'm too scared of him waking up. I don't want him to see me naked, in fact I don't want him to see me at all. So I lie here very still, holding the arm that's around me and hoping I'm playing this game right, hoping it will all be over soon . . .

. . . I'm left to the emptiness of my room in a bed now covered in the evidence of destruction. I turn my head to see a used condom hanging from a handle on my chest of drawers. I look down and see pale red stains on my legs and sheets. So it's true. I am no longer the virgin in white.

I put on my dressing gown and wash my face. I feel like a changed woman, aging quickly by the second. I make my bed and try to tidy my room, hoping to cover up any trace of what had occurred.

He's waiting downstairs with a spliff to calm my retching stomach. I throw up in the bathroom and bring my head into alignment with my present reality. It's over, get over it, go and be the beautiful woman he wants you to be. Don't make a big deal out of this.

And I did. I've got over it. I've accepted my new identity, my new dirty reality. I am the woman who was meant to be pure, who has always protected that and now it was gone in one fell swoop. And I am left empty with not even memories to tell a story.

Suddenly the life I knew came to a complete stop as I realized that my beautiful dream of maintaining purity had been shattered as the feeling of defilement surrounded me and I entered a world of shame. Over the following weeks and months I began to get help and welcomed a couple of people into my pain to try to reclaim what had been lost and stolen. Because I had shut down so much emotionally it took a while before I was able to even fully connect with everything that had been happening and it was a long time before I was able to cry about it. Throughout this time I always maintained that I had consented to sleeping with him because it was much easier to talk about it that way, but as time went on I questioned this more and more and the question 'was I raped?' began to swirl through my mind regularly.

17 July 2009

> I don't want to be an object but I feel like one.
> I want to be lovely and lovable but I don't feel it.
> I want to be treasured and protected but I feel vulnerable and alone.
> I shouldn't be here in this place, it was meant to be different, it was all meant to be different, to be perfect. I feel broken and used, like some discarded toy waiting to be resold.

In October I then went away for a month to Brazil to take a course on sexuality. I didn't realize that this time was going to be as much about God healing me as it was about me learning. It was probably one of the most intense months of my life as I experienced flashback after flashback, letting God remind me of things that I had forgotten from years previously.

The morning after my virginity was taken was one of the most broken times of my life. All hope had left me and I was sure that those dreams that I had carried for so long had been dashed once and for all. I had taken hold of the belief that the dreams of purity, of having a beautiful wedding and marriage one day down the line had gone, that they were no longer achievable. The result of that night had been to reduce me, in my mind's eye, to an object and nothing more. I had lost all trust in men and any advances that were made towards me actually made me angry, as I translated it as men believing that they had the right to look at me/ask me out/whistle from their car windows, simply because they were men. I was angry for quite some time.

But God began to whisper restoration and hope into my heart again during the following months and my time in Brazil. I began to let my heart open up and begin healing from the damage it had incurred. I was able to forgive each man that had hurt me and, instead of holding anger towards them, I was able to ask God to bless their lives and release us from the encounters that we had shared, which brought freedom to my heart. I now honestly hold no blame over them or feel that they owe me anything. I've been able to come to a place where my heart is free from the brokenness of those past encounters.

Whatever our life journeys look like it's quite likely that from time to time we'll encounter moments that damage our hearts, disappoint our dreams or cause us to feel hopeless about our futures. Overall I have a wonderful life but I have experienced these things and have then learnt how to pick up the pieces and not let them destroy me. Something that was key for me in moving forward was being able to dream again. I had let my dreams die following that night in May but that didn't need to be the end of the story. I began to remember the promises that God had spoken to me about my life, the dreams he had given me of working with women to see their lives restored. I began to turn to words of hope and encouragement and let them fill my mind rather than the voice of shame that told me I was a worthless mess.

27 July 2009

Fear rewrites history and I think so does disappointment and loneliness. They all rewrite history's victories and promises in an attempt to steer you away from the future. But I remember now. I remember now the promises God spoke to me and they have not changed. His love has not changed. His presence has not changed.

Beginning in Brazil, I entered a season of being led away by God so that he could tenderly restore me, my heart and my dreams. During this time I wrote the following poem to give voice to the cry of my heart to find restoration.

To Be Lost In Your Arms

I just want to be lost in your arms,
Let me lose myself in your love again.
Would you saturate my very being
and cause my mind to follow you?
Please let me know what love is,
my feeble heart has forgotten its touch.
I just want to be lost in your arms,
Let me lose myself in your love again.

I've felt like a dirty footprint
in freshly fallen snow.

Please would you cover me once more
and cause purity to envelop me.
Please would you restore this broken body,
mind and soul.
I just want to be lost in your arms,
Let me lose myself in your love again.

I do not feel worthy or deserving.
But I just want to be lost in your arms,
Let me lose myself in your love again.

And in his faithfulness God responded with this to my heart:

My beloved spoke and said to me,
Arise, my darling,
my beautiful one, come with me.
See! The winter is past;
the rains are over and gone.
Flowers appear on the earth;
the season of singing has come,
the cooing of doves
is heard in our land.
The fig-tree forms its early fruit;
the blossoming vines spread their fragrance.
Arise, come, my darling;
my beautiful one, come with me.'
(Song of Songs 2:10–13)

God completely restored my heart and my dreams and my
purity. My journey to this point hasn't been a walk in the park

but it's made me even more passionate about living a life of sexual purity and consecration and seeing every life restored.

Pearls:

Chloe

I recently took a friend of mine, who also happens to work in the red-light district in Liverpool, on a shopping trip to Tesco to get her weekly groceries. I have never enjoyed buying bread and milk so much! Throughout our entire car journey and time in the store, a big smile was spread across her face and a childlike skip could be seen in her walk. She was being loved and delighted in, just as she deserved to be. She hadn't done anything to earn a free grocery shop except that she was Chloe and she was worthy.

Chloe was passed from foster home to foster home throughout the UK from the age of 8 until she was 18 and cut loose from the system. During her time within the care system she was regularly sexually abused and became exposed far too young to the desires of men. Alcohol and drugs were made available to her, which helped to alleviate the memories that she was trying so hard to forget, and she was introduced to the ways of prostitution to ensure her new habit could be paid for.

Injustice latches on to the vulnerable and works quickly to sew a web around them that seems impossible to break; however, it doesn't have to win. Although Chloe is still working on the streets, her drug habit has a weaker hold on her than it once had and her heart has become increasingly opened to God, the one who loves her the most.

It is easy to look at a woman standing on a street corner and label them with one glance of an eye, judging them silently, before moving on. They haven't ended up there by accident, injustice has led them there and will keep them pinned to that pavement until someone who knows and lives by the truth is willing to approach them and love them because they are worthy and because it could just as easily have been us.

8

Broken by Beauty

It was about 27°C and already about 11 p.m. as I stood in the middle of a crack den in Vitória, Brazil. The main road that I was on was fairly empty of traffic but the streets and buildings that lined it were alive with human activity. I watched as a young boy ran between different men, passing small packages to and fro, before disappearing into a building across the street from me. Groups of men and women were hanging out in a courtyard area just down from where I was standing, the sound of drinking and conversations filling the air.

I was with a small group of men and women from a local centre called Avalanche Missões Urbanas. Avalanche's vision is to promote the expansion of the kingdom of God through Christian training, and developing interventions for the urban problems that are facing Brazil and the world. Every year they run several intensive schools in everything from sexuality to history and politics. In October 2009 I found myself in the heat of the Brazilian east coast, along with about twenty other young men and women, studying sexuality on an entirely Brazilian/Portuguese-speaking course; the only language I knew was English. Thankfully I was blessed to have a beautiful, English-speaking lady on the course with me who became my interpreter for the month and my communication lifeline.

Esther is originally from Switzerland but now lives in Brazil working with many victims of sexual abuse.

I was walking beside Esther on this evening as we began approaching some of the women who were working in the area to give out chocolates and simply let them know that they are loved. One of the main differences that I've found in working in red-light districts around the world is the presence of children. In Liverpool or Stoke for example I've never seen a child out working with the women but in Brazil, and Thailand as well, children were running around in the midst of it all, some of them helping with drug deals, others there because their mothers were working. A child's innocence isn't safe in such environments.

We began talking with a lady who was on the street, working to sell herself, who was about six months pregnant, her stomach bulging with twins. She became fascinated with me because of my white skin, blue eyes and blonde hair. Through Esther's translations we were able to have a small conversation and she told me about her unborn children, letting me touch her stomach. As she spoke about them she seemed to glow with the joy of motherhood and choose to ignore the barrenness of her surroundings. She then pulled me into a warm hug and asked me what my name was: 'Joy,' I replied. 'Joy: a beautiful name. I will call my daughter Joy like the girl from England.' She rubbed her stomach and looked at me, smiling. I felt stunned to have been given such an honour by this beautiful young woman and so wished I had the words to be able to communicate with her fully, but instead I held her, feeling her pregnancy against my own body and told her that I loved her.

16 October 2009

I went on outreach tonight and watched crack being distributed, smoked, snorted, bought, sold, begged for and sought after. About four of the women that we saw were pregnant, all still working the streets with bulging stomachs.

One of the street girls was pregnant with twins. She's going to name the girl 'Joy'.

I looked pain in the face tonight and it took my breath away.

There are certain experiences, moments, people and times that become significant landmarks in our lives. My month in Brazil was definitely one of those as I was welcomed into the Avalanche family with open arms and found a home in a place so foreign to my own upbringing. It was here that I gained greater revelation of God's original intention for sexuality and found restoration for my own sexual brokenness.

The idea of going to Brazil first came about in July 2009 when I went to Slot Art Festival in Lubiaz, Poland, with a team from my church in Liverpool. We went for the duration of the festival to run their 24/7 prayer room and facilitate creative spaces to pray and encounter God. During one sunny afternoon I was sat in one of the grassy open areas, sewing patches onto people's clothes that had words such as 'beautiful', 'chosen' and 'unique' written on them in Polish, when a big Brazilian man with several tattoos adorning his arms came over to me. Diniz's smile immediately gave away the cheeky warmth that I later learnt fills his heart and he began to speak to me in pidgin English and Spanish. Our conversation didn't get too far, however, as neither of us could really understand the other very well. Thankfully his wife, Andréa, then appeared who was fluent in English and began explaining where they were both from and their involvement with the festival.

Diniz and Andréa run Avalanche Missões Urbanas in the city of Vitória, Espirito Santo and their greatest attribute is love. As I stood there talking to Andréa she began to pour out her heart: 'I love the gays, the prostitutes, the transvestites, the sexually abused.' I loved this woman straight away. How often do we hear someone say those words to us as a simple outpouring of their heart? She began to tell me about a school of sexuality that they run at Avalanche every year and invited me to come. It was such a random encounter in many ways but it was one that caught my attention and stayed with me. I wanted to gain from this couple who carried such wealth in their hearts and so off to Brazil I went four months later.

I arrived in Vitória with no real idea of what to expect, or quite what the following month would hold, but with an earnest desire to learn and grow in this area of sexuality. I certainly wasn't expecting it to make me feel so vulnerable, or to be as personally stretching as it ended up being, but I'm so thankful that it was. The course covered topics such as sexual abuse and rape right through to the theology of sexuality and God's original intention for it. It was an intense few weeks but a course that I would recommend to anyone, particularly for those who want to work in this area.

15 October 2009

Tonight we had a class on the Theology of Sexuality and it blew my mind! To hear that the biggest area to receive destruction after the fall was sexuality was like a big light bulb being switched on for me. My view of sex recently has been that it destroys, that I just want it out of my life, out of this world. But actually it is good and has merely been subject to the aftermath of the fall. Even swear-words have been created to degrade sex.

Tonight I've felt a real restoration of my mind, a realigning of my thoughts on sex to how God thinks, to his original intentions.

I look back on so many of my sexual experiences and see how greatly they were distorted, how far they were from God's intentions; his design.

We were created in the image of God (Genesis 1:26) and for his glory. Everything about who we are – our bodies, our minds, our creativity, the way we live and love – was intended to mirror our Creator and bring glory to him. This includes our sexuality and relationships. Sex and its dysfunctions are not separate from God but involve him completely. He is the only one who can bring full restoration when we are broken, and it is through him that we are able to truly comprehend what it means to love with purity and honour.

Sex was intended to bring glory to God. It was created by God (Colossians 1:16), is subject to him (Ephesians

1:22) and is therefore able to be restored and made new by him (Revelation 21:5). It was never intended to be used to degrade or abuse, to bring shame or invoke feelings of pain. It was created for pleasure, for God's glory, for intimacy and for beauty. So how is it that for so many people, especially within the church, sex is something that is shameful to talk about, is embarrassing or brings up negative emotions?

Sex was designed by God that we might know more about who he is. We were created in his image, therefore every aspect of our make-up has been infiltrated by his design and character. If we were to study our bodies or the unique intellect that we all have, we would find arrows pointing to a God who is the source of this creation and has left clues everywhere that we might be able to find him, whether we are a scientist or an artist. Our sexuality has been formed by God and is meant to draw us deeper into intimacy with him rather than further away from that reality. As we grow deeper in intimacy with God, our sexuality is also able to come under his covering and be guided by him.

God and sex are not at war with each other, they are on the same team. It is Satan who is at war with God and therefore at war with our sexuality. Which part of our being comes under the most scrutiny, abuse, degradation and criticism? Our sexuality.

Satan knows the true value of our sexuality and he knows that if he can take that value away then he can keep us removed from intimacy, from pleasure and from purity. Over the last fifty years in particular, the value of sex has dropped and it continues to do so. There is evidence of this in everything from our movies and commercials to our language, humour

and the explosion of the sex industry. Sex trafficking is quickly
becoming the world's most lucrative trade. A common phrase
that is used by those in advertising and in the media is that
'sex sells'. Unfortunately it does. Sex has become a commod-
ity available to anyone at the right price. We have become
very good at degrading sex without even realizing it.

Value needs to return to that which God values. Purity
needs to become more desirable than the temptation before
us.

The week after having spent my evening talking to street
sex workers in a crack den, I again found myself on the streets
of Vitória late at night on outreach. On this particular evening
we met four beautiful girls who were aged between 14 and 16
and had travelled from a nearby city to work for the evening.
I don't know the full extent of their story, as again it was lost
in translation to me, but I understood that they had come to
Vitória to sell themselves. After stopping and chatting to the
girls for a bit, the group that I was with decided to take them
back to our base and arrange for their transport back home
and to safety.

None of the four girls could speak English, and there
wasn't much that I could communicate in Portuguese, but
as we walked home they flanked my sides, holding my hands
and smiling up at me with their beautiful brown eyes. I think
I again won some favouritism with my English skin and
blonde hair but I didn't mind a bit. I spent the rest of my
evening with the girls, sat on cushions playing with make-up
and telling them how amazing and beautiful they were.

I don't know where those girls are now or how their stories
have panned out since that night in October 2009, but I

do know that for one night they were saved from having to exploit themselves, they were loved with no ulterior motives attached and were told over and over again the truth about their worth and identity. I believe in those moments. I believe in those encounters that may seem small when placed on the timeline of our lives, but that matter and impact beyond what we may ever come to know or understand.

One of the valuable life lessons that I uncovered at a deeper level in Brazil, and continue to now, is the power of forgiveness. Towards the end of my time in Vitória I spent some time with Andréa, sharing my heart and what had been brought up for me personally through taking the course. After listening to me for a while she responded with, 'I think you need to be able to forgive yourself.'

3 November 2009

On Saturday morning I finally managed to sit down and talk with Andréa. I shared with her all that God had been bringing up for me personally during the course and talked a lot about my history, my story. She said that I really needed to be able to forgive myself. I need to be able to look at myself and face how I really am; how I really feel. I need to look at myself face to face and see the truth. As of yet I haven't done that and I think I'm scared to. The thought is sitting at the back of my mind waiting to be acted upon.

Prior to going to Brazil, I had spent a lot of time processing what other people had done to me and coming to a place of being able to forgive them, releasing both them and myself from being attached to that wrong event forever. However, I found it much harder to be able to forgive myself and detach from the lies that I saw every time that I looked in the mirror. Over the years I had become very good at holding on to moments and memories simply because I had not been able to forgive myself for where I had gone wrong, and felt that I deserved to be punished for it.

9 December 2009

Dear Joy,

I know that this is me writing to myself but if I direct this at someone I may actually be able to finish it, it may actually come off of the page.

I remember things about you now from when you were a lot younger . . .

. . . I've become afraid of love, of commitment, of relationship. They are all things I want but they are not trustworthy anymore and therefore the price of loneliness seems somewhat worth it.

How can I be ready to love someone when I have not yet fully committed to loving myself? I need the young girl inside me to be embraced, told she is full of worth, loved and beautiful. Because I think the woman here is still trying to create that for her.

My month in Avalanche did wonders for my heart, as aside from the daily classes and weekly outreach, I was able to live alongside a group of incredible men and women who were all humbly working out their own brokenness with a desire to see others restored. Whether they realized it or not, their openness to love me taught me how to love myself again and brought me to a place where I could face up to the thoughts and memories from which I had been hiding. When I arrived back in England I took the time out to finally write to myself, admitting many things that I had been too afraid to put into words, and coming that bit closer to a whole heart.

> *Then I acknowledged my sin to you and did not cover up my*
> *iniquity. I said, 'I will confess my transgressions to the LORD.'*
> *And you forgave the guilt of my sin.*
> *(Psalm 32:5)*

The Bible is riddled with accounts of God's forgiveness towards humanity and his command to humnkind to continue forgiving. The very act of Jesus' death and resurrection was an act of forgiveness: forgiveness of sin. The whole of humanity was shown the greatest act of grace when Jesus died on the cross. Through the shedding of his blood we received forgiveness for every wrong thing that we have done and God has now handed us that same grace, that forgiveness, so that we might pass it on. It is one of the most powerful acts of freedom that we can undertake.

I cannot separate myself from the woman that I met, who was pregnant with twins and working to sell herself, or the young street girls that I spent my evening with. My heart is no more precious than theirs and my dreams and visions are no more valuable. We've all encountered moments of abuse, our hearts have all been overlooked and not held with care and we have all made decisions with consequences that have led to pain. Above all of those things though, God has offered each of us the hand of freedom and called us out of the darkness and into the light.

There have been many accounts in the UK, and I'm sure worldwide as well, of people in positions of authority regarding the life of someone working in prostitution as of lesser value than those who aren't. Many men and women who have been sleeping rough or found themselves working in the sex industry have died without so much as a record of it or a fight on their behalf. Every heart is valuable, every story is worthy of being told and some of the most beautiful hearts can be found residing in the body of a woman on the street corner.

9

Dreams Fulfilled

My phone started ringing and I stepped outside the bar that I was working in to answer it. It was my colleague from Pure, Abi Nevill, on the other end of the line: 'Joy, you did it, you won the funding!'

About six months previously a friend of mine had shown me an advert in *Glamour* magazine asking for people to submit their dreams and visions with a chance to win up to £10,000 to make them happen. There are normally several dreams on my radar that I want to see fulfilled, but in 2010 it was a particular desire to see freedom for young people struggling with self-harm and disordered eating that was taking up my focus.

A seed of this vision had first appeared in my heart when I was about 15. I remember being sat in the bathroom in our home in Stoke-on-Trent. I had just cut myself and was in the process of cleaning everything up, when I told myself that one day this would all be over, one day I would be free and one day I would be able to help other young people who were struggling in this area. Ever since that moment that was stark with my own brokenness, I wanted to make sure that this issue was talked about and that I could help where I could.

Since joining Pure in 2008, I had been happily telling my story of finding freedom and breaking the cycle of self-harm, but we were increasingly seeing a need to do more than just tell young people about a journey of hope: we also wanted to invite them into one. It's great to be able to start a conversation with people about issues that they are struggling with, and otherwise wouldn't have a safe context to unpack it in, but it's also important to not just leave people with an open can of worms but to also offer a solution. We began talking about this as a team at Pure and soon we highlighted a gap that needed to be filled. We needed to be offering further help to young people once they had acknowledged that issues such as self-harm were a problem for them.

I am a big believer in the restorative value of creativity and love using it as a key that unlocks freedom, breakthrough and hope for those who choose to access it. With this in mind, Abbie Hosier (the Health Promotions Manager for Pure) and I formed a vision together for a proposed twelve-week group mentorship project named Pure Freedom to which young people could be referred, where they could unpack the roots behind their coping mechanisms using medical advice and creative tools as a form of therapy.

In the spring of 2010 I then decided to take a risk and put forward Pure Freedom as a vision that deserved funding from *Glamour* magazine. I was stunned to have the project short-listed by the judges for a public vote and in July 2010 I received the phone call that informed me that it had come out top in its category and was being awarded £5,000!

This was an amazing achievement for the team at Pure and enabled Pure Freedom to be launched in Liverpool to begin supporting young people in a more comprehensive way, but it was also the fulfilment of my own personal dream. I always believed that my own broken story could be redeemed but I had not imagined that it would come with such public support.

16 May 2010

You have dust on your clothes, you've been rolling around in other people's ashes. But I, God, will blow on you, I will blow on you now, and as I blow all ashes are given back to the wind.

You should only be rolling around in my dust, in my gold dust from heaven. That is what was made to linger on your skin because your skin is precious to me. Do you see that, do you understand? I placed my glory within you, amongst the layers of your skin. So be coated in me, in my promises, in my dreams and visions for you, in the richness of my presence.

It was in this time of seeing the vision of Pure Freedom birthed that God began speaking to me a lot about restoration in my own life. I began to see how he had restored my creativity to be something that brought life and beauty rather than displaying reflections of darkness. I found myself in a season of him blowing fresh life over me, ridding me from the cobwebs of the past.

There have been several words of encouragement that I have received over the last few years, and held on to as promises. They have served to keep me going when things have felt particularly hard. It is so easy to focus on what has happened in the past, what we've done or what has been done to us, that it is sometimes hard to look forward without tainted vision. I have found this passage from Isaiah to be a source of encouragement and also a declaration that my past does not need to control my future.

Forget the former things;
do not dwell on the past.
See, I am doing a new thing!
Now it springs up; do you not perceive it?
I am making a way in the wilderness
and streams in the wasteland.
The wild animals honour me,
the jackals and the owls,
because I provide water in the wilderness
and streams in the wasteland,
to give drink to my people, my chosen,
the people I formed for myself
that they may proclaim my praise.
(Isaiah 43:18–21)

I entered 2010 with a desire to leave 2009 firmly in the past and saw the New Year as an opportunity for a fresh start. I had received so much healing in my heart through my time in Brazil, and the investment of people close to me in Liverpool, but I still had my wobbles; I still had to endure regular flashbacks and my heart did still ache from time to time when I looked at what I had lost. Therefore Isaiah 43 became a bit of a lifeline passage for me that I learnt off by heart and would encourage myself with in those moments. Restoration became my buzz word and soon filled my vision. I wanted full restoration of my past. I wanted to see all things in me made new.

28 December 2009

The year 2010 is going to be a year of restoration and of purity. There is an advance that will take place as cords are broken and tethers are cut. There is an acceleration that is about to take place. It's going to start at the core, the roots. No longer will you walk on the cracks of broken ground but your feet will tread on ground that will not be shaken, on ground that will not be moved.

I began reading stories about how God had restored people's lives in the Bible and became hooked on one in particular, the story of Hosea. Hosea was a man of God who took a lady, Gomer, to be his wife after God told him to. Gomer was working as a prostitute when they met and during their marriage would continue to run away to work but Hosea would go after her, searching every back alley until he found her. He didn't give up on her but brought her home and loved her. That love restored her and placed her identity in truth. She was Hosea's wife, not a prostitute. Her heart was worthy to be loved, not to be paid for over and over by random men.

'Therefore I am now going to allure her;
I will lead her into the wilderness
and speak tenderly to her.

There I will give her back her vineyards,
and will make the Valley of Achor a door of hope.
There she will respond as in the days of her youth,
as in the day she came up out of Egypt.

'In that day,' declares the LORD,
'you will call me "my husband",
you will no longer call me "my master". . .
. . . I will betroth you to me for ever;
I will betroth you in righteousness and justice,
in love and compassion.
I will betroth you in faithfulness,
and you will acknowledge the LORD.'
(Hosea 2:14–16,19,20)

This spoke so much life to my heart when I first read it, and it still does. Those wilderness periods can often be seen as a negative time, or can at least feel like one, as a weaker version of ourselves is presented to the world. However, we didn't end up there by accident, or because we took a wrong turn, we were instead gently led by our Father so that he might tenderly speak to our hearts, reaffirming the truth about who we are and restoring the brokenness that we've been experiencing. It doesn't matter how messed up things may have become, how far we think that we have fallen or what our life may look like; it doesn't have to stay that way. We are invited to sever our ties with brokenness and become betrothed to the one who is love, whose love restores and makes new, who heals and never abandons.

Although it is painful, the time we spend in the wilderness can actually be one of the most precious seasons. I've found that it is during those times where I have felt at my weakest that hope has also seemed the most alive, and I've been able to treasure beauty in a way that I would not have done if I hadn't had to enter that season. The wilderness can also be a time where vision is sharpened and renewed.

The story of Hosea, and this passage in particular, is one that I meditated on for a long time, soaking in its restorative truth and letting it speak hope into my heart for the future. I began to find purpose in this time as I encouraged myself with the thought that I was not walking through this season in vain, I would one day be able to use these experiences to help others, to help other women who had become the victims of sexual exploitation. My vision for what I would do with my life began to grow and my passion to see restoration within the area of sexuality and relationships expanded. Soon the fire within me that was desperate for change and hot with righteous anger at the thought of how many people were currently being robbed of their innocence worldwide and held captive by abuse and shame, began to spur me through my own season of restoration and healing and straight into the arms of wholeness.

The launch of Pure Freedom for me symbolized a shift in the course of my life. It was a declaration that those whispered words of hope and vision, spoken out from places of captivity, are not uttered in vain but will come to pass. Words create worlds and in this case a door of freedom was established.

As restoration was found within the work that I was doing with my hands, and the Pure Freedom project took shape for its launch in 2011, the area of my heart also began to see new life. My dear friend Sarah, who I had taken the Silver Ring

Thing pledge with years before, celebrated her 21st birthday in June 2010. I travelled down to Devon to spend some time with her and her family in a place that is very dear to my heart, and over the years has been a haven for healing, where I have felt known, loved and safe. Sarah's birthday celebrations then became combined with the news that she was now engaged to Dave, her childhood sweetheart. My heart was filled with joy as I watched my amazing friend taking that first step of a lifetime commitment with the answer of 'yes'. I later took part in their wedding day as a very proud bridesmaid and watched as she married her Hub!

During that visit I spent an afternoon with Sarah's parents, Chris and Kerry, who over the years have given much valuable input into my family's life and mine. As we sat in their wood-adorned attic, they gently began to ask me about areas of my heart that I had not openly talked about in a while or even allowed myself to think about. I was surprised at first but I trusted their lead and soon we began to talk about my relationship with Phillip and the possibility that there might still be a future for us both. Up until this point I had become completely closed to this idea, and as a way to protect my heart, had put all hope of a restoration with Phillip in a locked box far away.

A couple of hours after we had first sat down with a cup of tea, we prayed together, surrendering our conversation to God and asking that his will would be done in both my life and in Phillip's. A month and a half later saw us being reunited in the city of Stoke-on-Trent where we had first met. Our mutual friend, Mark, was getting married and we were both invited to attend the full day of celebrations with Phillip dancing in the ceremony. Two days before the wedding I was sat in Costa trying to concentrate on reading and settling my stomach as I waited for Phillip to arrive. I was unsure what to expect and probably even less sure of how I would react to seeing him again.

Phillip arrived, a warm smile spreading across his face as he greeted me and pulled out exactly the same book that I was reading from his bag, plonking it down on the table next to mine. 'We're reading the same book!'

I smiled but found myself feeling a little annoyed at the common ground that had already appeared, and I inwardly felt for the guards of self-protection to make sure that they were firmly up. I didn't want to get hurt again and no matter how beautiful his smile may be I didn't want to trust it yet.

We sat opposite each other, my mug of Earl Grey tea and his large mocha taking place on the table between us. The conversation slowly warmed up from greetings and turned into apologies as our conversation travelled back to the previous year and brought closure to that chapter in our tale. I wasn't ready to let my heart become completely open, however, and so I continued to sit with it well guarded as Phillip began to openly share his. '. . . I feel like there is further for us to journey together. We didn't get the chance to discover it last year, but the possibility is worth investing in . . .'

My heart and mind became a whirlwind and I tried to keep my face neutral as I listened to the words that he spoke so eloquently. Would I consider coming out to California and seeing if this is just friendship between us or a marriage? I heard the question but didn't quite believe it and felt my stomach doing the washing machine manoeuvre as I tried to process the proposal and at the same time maintain control of every part of me.

My immediate response of course was no, no way. There was no way I was about to move to another city, in another country, when there was so much that was beginning to open up and come to life where I was. I felt whole, alive, full of hope and vision and I didn't want to lose this new ground that I had found. Added to this was the secret knowledge that only I knew. He didn't know what had occurred in the space in-between us having last seen each other and if he knew he would probably change his mind anyway. These were the thoughts that swirled through my mind as I sat in my room that night replaying the whole conversation and trying to figure out what I was meant to do.

It was then that I heard that beautiful still, small voice and felt the presence of peace that I have learnt to view as my compass in moments of confusion or trial. 'Truth. Let yourself be honest with him and tell him the truth.' I'm definitely all for truth but following what is right and true often leads to some really hard and uncomfortable conversations.

The day following our initial reunion found us meeting up again in Hanley, where we sat on a bench outside the Potteries Museum and I allowed myself to indeed speak the truth. I was scared to say it out loud, scared of what the response may be; scared that the little flame of hope that had begun to grow overnight might be blown out again. I needn't have feared. Phillip sat there and listened, his eyes soft to my story and his responding words full of grace with not even the merest taint of condemnation or a change in his proposition.

That decision to choose truth rather than the temptation to flee brought a greater level of freedom to my heart, bringing further destruction to shame and allowing that flame of hope to begin to steadily grow. Although I still hadn't made a decision, by the end of the weekend and my return journey to Liverpool I had come to the point where my response to Phillip's invitation had become 'yes'.

Two weeks later I met up with Phillip again in Edinburgh, a city that I hadn't returned to since our break-up, and told him that my answer was yes. I wanted to continue the journey with him, whatever that ended up looking like and wherever that ended up taking us. We became 'friends with a promise', not wanting to rush into anything but committing ourselves to rebuilding our friendship and finding a context where we could do life in the same place.

When I had sat on the sofa in Chris and Kerry's attic I had not imagined that this level of restoration could take place. I had let my heart become softer to the idea of it being a possibility but hadn't dared to hope that it could evolve into a reality. Two months later I found myself saying yes to a new journey with an old friend. How beautiful is the faithfulness of God that he is able to restore all things, even when we have given up on them?

On 4 January 2011 Phillip again became my boyfriend as we walked through the city of Redding, California during a visit I made that year. On Saturday, 17 March 2012, as the sun broke out over Pasadena Bridge in Los Angeles, the love of my life knelt down on one knee and asked me to be his wife.

I have liked Phillip since I first met him as a 17-year-old and when things went awry in 2009 I came to a point where I never thought things could be restored in my life and made new. I agreed with the lie that from this point on life would be second best and I was not worthy of the 'happily ever after.' My journey since then has completely destroyed that thought and called it out for what it is – rubbish. God has restored my dreams. He has restored my relationship with Phillip and caused it to be ten times stronger than it had been the first time. He has restored my past and turned events that left me in ashes to be moments that bring glory to this earth and the heavens.

Forget the former things;
do not dwell on the past.
See, I am doing a new thing!
Now it springs up; do you not perceive it?
(Isaiah 43:18,19)

7 November 2010

Do you ever look up?
I mean really look up?
Do you ever gaze at the skies with questions in your eyes,
Staring at the expanse of oceans above you, wondering which
cloud is yours?

Or maybe you love sand,
spending hours filtering the grains in your hand,
watching the world at your feet.

But grains do not tell of the glories of the sky,
they speak but of the past, the present, with no eyes for the
future
Sand is but of the moment.
Take your gaze higher and wider,
let your eyes behold more than your toes can feel,
Breathe in the open skies!

There are so many mysteries resting just above your head,
so many expanses yet unknown,
stories untold,
wonders unimagined.

I dare you to take a moment and lift your gaze,
Look higher, further, wider, beyond
Take in the mysteries of the open skies and fill them with your
dreams.
Crouch, ready and expectant, for the great unveiling,
The unravelling of your part in the story.

Behold the promises within your grasp.
Behold the mysteries unimagined that have been created just for
you.

Pearls:

Jennie

We were walking along the beach, Jennie and I, trying to shield ourselves from the biting cold wind when she asked whether I knew her story. I knew snippets, but most of it was a mystery to me. I responded with a no, giving her permission to share as much as she wanted.

As Jennie began to speak, her arm linked through mine, a fresh love and compassion filled my heart. She was the only child to parents who later divorced and from the age of 5 was sexually abused by her dad. This abuse carried on for years and when she was 15 she fell pregnant by him. Jennie decided that she couldn't keep the child and had an abortion. Soon after all of this she decided to move away and ended up in Liverpool living with a guy who was horrendously abusive to her. Alcohol became the friend on which she was dependent, drugs helped her to forget the pain, and prostitution allowed her to pay for both. For a while she lived on the streets but for the past couple of years she had been living in a hostel.

A couple of weeks before our blustery walk along the beach I had come to pick up Jennie from her hostel to take her to church. She hadn't had a very easy week as her best friend hadn't been well and had had to go to hospital. That Sunday, however, she had found out that her friend was being discharged and sent home. In her excitement she went out and worked to earn enough money to buy her friend some flowers.

I was stunned by this act of love that Jennie had made with no thought or concern for her own welfare. A gift that would be so easy for me to purchase at the value of a few pounds, became priceless as it was offered from her hands. A bunch of flowers should never have to cost the price of a woman's body.

Jennie is a good friend of mine and is now a member of the same church as me. In a lot of ways life is really hard for her right now but she also has more hope than she ever had before. This pearl is discovering her true identity and beginning to shrug off the lies that have been repeated to her all her life. She is now looking to start voluntary work with the church and has stopped drinking. The journey hasn't ended, but hope has her held firmly by the hand.

10

Strip Bars & Prayer Rooms

5 September 2011

So here I am in JFK and this is really happening, I'm really moving to another continent for a boy! I don't even have a job to pin to me. I am completely free, totally released. And surprisingly I don't feel much, it actually feels quite normal!

Moving house was not a new phenomenon to me but transitioning to LA from Liverpool was the first time that it had been my choice, not because my parents were there but because I was choosing to invest in my own family. I had moments of anxiety that would send my stomach into butterflies but for the most part I was just excited. For the first time since I'd met Phillip we wouldn't have to say goodbye to each other after a couple of days, we could just be a normal couple enjoying life together.

I had managed to wrap up my busy life in Liverpool over the couple of months running up to my departure and threw a big party for all of my friends and family to say goodbye. I've never been a fan of goodbyes and have always tried to avoid them as best I can; however I seem to have chosen a lifestyle that makes them a regular occurrence.

My first twenty-four hours in LA felt a little wobbly for me as my heart grieved the distance that I felt between where I was now and everything that I had always known, loved and called home. However, as day two dawned just as clear, bright and sunny as the first, my heart settled and I smiled: this was my new home.

Before leaving England I had had no idea of what I would be doing, how I would fill my time or even where I would live long term. After less than a week of being in the city of Los Angeles I had a potential new housemate and had been asked to intern for a school of ministry that was based at a house of prayer in Pasadena. Not for the first time in my life I found myself floored by the goodness and faithfulness of God.

My day-to-day life began to look very different to how it had ever looked before as I began regularly attending meetings and prayer slots in the Pasadena International House of Prayer (PIHOP). I have always had a high value for prayer and a desire to carve out time to spend worshipping God and listening for what he has to say, but I have never before been a part of a community that literally creates a space for that every day. Countless books, talks and conferences have been held over the years on the importance of establishing a lifestyle of prayer but nothing really preaches it like living it out for real. I soon found myself spoilt with the amount of input I was receiving, and flourishing in my zeal for the supernatural and a tangible sense of God's presence. I thoroughly enjoyed the freedom of not having to work sixty- to seventy-hour weeks like I had been doing, and to instead be able to invest in relationships, in myself and in my own walk with God.

I've discovered over the last few years that one of my strengths is that I'm an activator. I like to be on the go, getting things done, turning what is written down from words into reality. If I see that something needs to be done or changed then I'll do it. I don't like to sit around thinking about it all for long; I want to make it happen! On the flip side of this strength is the tendency to say yes to everything, to start a million projects all at once because you see need wherever you look, and the result is that you end up burnt out and no help to anyone. My strength as an activator is still something that I'm learning how to manage as I can find seasons where I seem to be doing 'nothing' very challenging and I get the urge to get up and do. This was a recurring reaction to my sudden change in lifestyle pace as I adjusted to being in LA and away from my well established life and position in Liverpool.

A couple of weeks after I arrived in Pasadena, Los Angeles, I attended a viewing of a new documentary film called *Nefarious: Merchant of Souls* that was being shown at PIHOP. I had heard about the making of the film for the past year or so and was excited that my arrival in America coincided with the start of its US tour. *Nefarious* unveils the truth behind international modern-day sex slavery and, in the space of a couple of hours, takes you on a journey around the world to see the nightmare of sex slavery that thousands of men, women and children are experiencing daily. Watching the film broke my heart afresh, reigniting my passion to fight injustice, and also gave me hope that change is possible and we can break this cycle of human slavery.

19 September 2011

Last night I watched *Nefarious: Merchant of Souls* at a showing at PIHOP.
Powerful.

Following the documentary we had a time of intercession for the worldwide issue of human trafficking. It was a time that I didn't want to be pulled out of. There was such unity in the spirit and a real tangible sense of God's presence as we cried out to him for justice.

For me I felt the evening to be a recommissioning to work in the area of justice and restoration. I know that I was created to see the abolition of slavery and the restoration of purity once more.

Two of the Scriptures that were prayed into are the ones that I have tattooed on my body: Amos 5 and Isaiah 61: words that have become the mandate for my life.

> *But let justice roll on like a river,*
> *righteousness like a never-failing stream!*
> *(Amos 5:24)*

> *He has sent me to bind up the brokenhearted,*
> *to proclaim freedom for the captives*
> *and release from darkness for the prisoners,*
> *to proclaim the year of the Lord's favour*
> *and the day of vengeance of our God,*

> *to comfort all who mourn,*
> *and provide for those who grieve in Zion*
> *to bestow on them a crown of beauty instead of ashes,*
> *the oil of joy*
> *instead of mourning,*
> *and a garment of praise*
> *instead of a spirit of despair.*
> *They will be called oaks of righteousness,*
> *a planting of the* LORD *for the display of his splendour.*
> *(Isaiah 61:1–3)*

My eyes began to be opened afresh to the powerful marriage between prayer and justice. If you're anything like me and you find yourself in the 'doing' category, then sometimes it can be easy to bypass the place of prayer and see it as having less importance than a night of outreach or a meeting with leaders. In actual fact prayer needs to be at the foundation of every step that we make and is the bow from which our arrows of justice should be released. Keeping this regular conversation with God open can be a challenge, and it is a discipline that I think we often have to teach ourselves rather than being one that necessarily comes very naturally. We were created for relationship with our Creator though and prayer is just one facet of how to keep that connection fresh and alive.

For justice to be 100 per cent successful I believe that we need the backing of heaven and the only way to achieve that is to ask for it. The Bible is full of God's desire to see justice and righteousness reign in this earth, so we need not be afraid that he would say no to our requests to bring it.

As I found myself in this season of peace where demands were not constantly being made on my time, God began to impress on me the idea of 'selah'. Selah means to weigh; to value; to pause or meditate; to stop and listen. As I began to study this idea in more depth, I felt God highlight the importance of valuing this principle of selah, of having selah moments where we pause, stop and value the presence of God. This principle has eternal value in it, it is not for just one season, it's for a lifetime.

What if we were to be heralds of the value of 'selah'? Imagine if we could be men and women with sacred and inviolable character whose lives show that they have an intimate relationship with God; who pause to meditate on the word of God and value his presence forever; men and women who have the ear and attention of the commanders of armies, nations and kingdoms. I believe that 'selah' is a principle of heaven that we can learn and cultivate now. A selah moment can appear as we are challenged or convicted, as we praise God or find ourselves in mourning, rejoicing or in times of questioning. God's presence can still enter in, no matter what our circumstance.

The fire of God's presence is released and burns hotter within us the more that we take time to value it. Fire burns up the dross and enables us to see more clearly; it releases fresh vision and boldness to push forward in what God is calling us to do. In its wake are increased answers to prayer, peace, strength, revelation and increased wisdom. It creates purity of heart and mind. As we allow ourselves to be consumed with his fire, through cultivating his presence, our tongues are released to speak what is on his heart.

This principle has now become the foundation of how I personally want to seek out justice on this earth, from a posture of being in the presence of God. It is now a non-negotiable for me that every act of outreach and moving forward in vision be backed by heaven and soaked in God's presence. I believe that by choosing to engage in the supernatural, we are able to gain greater levels of freedom and restoration in people's lives. There have been many times when I have been in conversation with friends, family and people that I have randomly met when I have suddenly had deeper insight into what is going on in their lives. You may call this discernment, wisdom or just being able to read people well but I believe that the more that I lean into God and am open to listening to his voice, the more he will reveal things to me even if that is something as small as having a little more insight into someone's life.

The more time that I invested in prayer, the sharper my ability became to be able to hear what God was saying, but I also came away with more questions about the amount of injustice there is in the world. Following my time in Thailand I had more questions than before pouring out of me and I battled with them for quite a while as my heart, that had become so broken by all it had witnessed, took time to find safety again.

3 February 2012

Every day on the streets of Bangkok we would walk to the store, the market, a coffee shop or a meeting place and pass families living on the streets; begging for survival. People with limbs missing, bodies riddled with leprosy, babies with no home. One guy in particular would always wrench at my heart when I passed him. He was lying face down on the pavement with an arm outstretched in front of him holding a cup for people to throw their spare change into. I think one of his legs was missing, at least his feet were I think. He would push himself along on his belly up and down the pavement all day long. I never saw his face, it was always facing the ground. And every day we just walked past him, sometimes even stepping over him to get past. Why did I never stop? Why did I never ask him what his name is, pick him up and look into his eyes, giving him the respect, honour and dignity that he deserves? Why didn't I offer to pray for him or even pull out some money from my western traveller's purse? Where is the justice for that man face down on the pavement? How did humanity become so broken and cold that we don't even stop to help pick up a body reduced to shame and humiliation?

Every day I walked by.

I don't want to walk by anymore. I don't want to live in a world where there is such brokenness, loneliness, poverty and shame. I want to embrace the hurting and offer love and hope. I want to be someone who stops, cares and looks each individual in the eyes because everybody deserves respect. Everybody is loved by the Father.

But God, if everybody is loved by you, how come so many of your children are being abused and going without? As soon as I ask it there are a million replies that jump to mind and cause me to wish that I had never asked, but sometimes those replies just don't seem good enough.

What good do I do sat in a prayer room as another young Thai girl is bought by an old white man? How does this really help everyone lost and trapped in Nana Plaza?

I've become one of those people haunted by the sights, sounds and faces of a foreign yet familiar land. What is seen in garish neon lights on the streets of Nana, Soi Cowboy and Pataya is found behind closed doors in the unseen world of porn, strip bars and sexual brokenness.

I don't want to keep my time in Thailand to just that, a two week church missions trip. I want to carry on living in the strip bars, loving the prostitutes, keeping my eyes open to what's really going on.

I don't want to become angry and hard, judgmental of the men or passive towards the women. I want to be soft with God's heart, quick to love and slow to anger.

My journal is full of questions following my time in Thailand and I really had to battle with how spending day and night in a house of prayer fits in with bringing men and women out of the captivity of sexual addiction and exploitation. This is one of those many things that I love about God: he is not afraid of our questions. As I walked through the season following my time in Thailand, I let

God hold my heart full of questions and listened as he gently spoke to me.

God wants us to partner with him to see justice reign on this earth. He is not a dictator but is a loving father, even more eager to see this earth in peace than we are. He refuses to force himself on us and instead invites us to hold his hand and walk into the dark places from a place of intimacy. The hours spent in a prayer room are just as valid and important as the night of outreach to show love to men and women in the sex industry. In fact we need to be men and women whose wells go deep so that people are able to draw from us in those moments of encounter.

In Revelation 8 it talks about the prayers of the saints, the people of God, being like incense that is sent up before the throne of God. In response to this intercession, fire is hurled down from heaven to earth with peals of thunder, rumblings, flashes of lightning and an earthquake. This could be interpreted literally but I also think that it reveals God's quickness to respond to our cries with his thundering breakthrough. He does not just sit upon his throne twiddling his thumbs but he responds with action, with justice, with resounding deliverance.

Action follows and goes hand in hand with prayer. Prayer is not wasted time or breath; it should not be squeezed into a corner of our day but should be the fuel behind our day-to-day movements and our greatest endeavours.

The weekend before Valentine's Day, I went out with a group of amazing young women to visit seven different strip bars in LA. We met up prior to going out together to put together gift bags for the women that we would be meeting, filled with make-up, cookies and messages of love. Our aim for the evening was to let the women know that they are loved and totally worth a gift on Valentine's Day. Before leaving the house we spent about an hour together praying and preparing our hearts for the places that we were about to enter, making sure that we were spiritually covered before doing anything else. Having that time together as a team and uniting under prayer dispelled any sense of fear and reminded us all of who is in control and who has the victory.

It can be very easy when we are going into intense environments, or coming up against establishments that seem so strong and impenetrable, to give in to fear or believe that it is not possible to see change. However, greater power is released and revealed when we choose to come together, not just physically but spiritually as well. By agreeing together that our God is greater and the powers of hell will not prevail against us, we are allowing the fire of heaven to be released onto earth and burn up that which sets itself up against the kingdom of heaven.

That night of outreach really touched me as we met many women who were working in the strip bars and were able to inject their evening with an encounter with pure love. One woman came running up to me in one of the bars asking if she could have a bag. I handed one to her with a smile and she asked why we were giving them the gifts. 'Because you are totally worth it and we want you to know that you are loved and we are thinking of you this Valentine's Day,' came my response.

She looked up from the bag in her hands and set her gaze directly on my eyes. 'Thank you so much!' I briefly glimpsed beyond the heavy make-up and glitzy attire into a heart that was young, innocent, crying out for love and trapped in a world of false promises and false love. I opened my arms and welcomed her into a warm hug before she had to scurry off to continue working. I wanted to have more time with her, to hear her story and listen to her, to respond with love and impart truth to her but instead I planted a seed, I took the two minutes I was given and gave her love, leaving her with a message that she is not forgotten.

Prayer paves the way for those encounters; it is the constant seed that is being sown in the spirit to be reaped in places like the dressing room of a strip club in LA.

Pearls:

June

June was a glorious pearl whose life has inspired and encouraged many people around her. She was also the best friend of another of my pearls, Jennie.

I first got to know June about four or five years ago. She was working on the streets in Liverpool and became a regular to the Streetwise van as she realized that the volunteers that she met there had a genuine love and care for her. It wasn't long before June began expressing how much she wanted out of this life; she didn't want to be working on the streets: she wanted a better way of living. She began coming along to church and soon gave her life to God, asking that he would help to change her and the way that she lived. June soon became the biggest evangelist for God and church, inviting everyone that she met and lived with to get to know God.

June was an absolute delight to know and always inspired me with her hunger to know God more and see her friends and family get to know him too. She was never afraid to speak her mind and had a laugh that filled a room with great joy.

On 8 January 2013 June passed away in her sleep at home and went to be with God whom she loves so much. She now gets to spend eternity in God's presence with her earthly sorrows far removed and laughter constantly at her lips. She has left behind a beautiful legacy of someone who never gave up, even though it would have been far easier for her to do so at times, but who carried on trusting in God, that he had the best for her. As with many of these pearls, her life had been riddled with abuse, neglect, addiction and disappointment but she was able to surrender this pile of ashes and receive a glorious crown of beauty in return.

It is because of June that Jennie is now such a good friend of mine and it is also because of her that many other pearls have been discovered and come to know a God who adores them completely.

11

Let Justice Flow

My life so far has been far from boring and is still continuing to unfold even as I type out these words. It has brought me to this current place of sitting and pondering on these many areas of injustice and what God might have in store for me to do next.

There are days when I can be completely overwhelmed by the amount of injustice in the world. It is everywhere that I look, on the television, on the radio, in the lives of my friends, in the minds of my family; it fills our magazines and newspapers and pulls on our heartstrings during two-minute commercials. I passionately hate injustice and there have been many times that I have had to stop watching a programme or reading an article and instead look upwards to God, who is the bringer of justice, so that my vision may be filled with his hope again rather than brought down by the negative sounds and visuals.

I seem to find injustices unavoidable as I go through each day and often struggle with how much I should open my mouth to speak against it; or when the right time is to step aside and let justice have its moment to speak. I was sat in the staffroom at work recently and picked up a women's magazine that was lying around. I started reading an article about a woman who had been able to break free from a cycle of prostitution that had been running through her family for five generations. It was amazing to hear of her breakthrough and also tragic to learn of the broken lives that had gone before her and the upper hand that injustice had seemed to have in this family. Just two pages after this was an article of sex tips from 'bad men', encouraging S&M-style adventures in the bedroom. My mind began to protest at the juxtaposition of the two articles and the apparent insensitivity of the editor to place them so closely together in a way that seemed to nullify what had been written about in the first article. It is in these seemingly insignificant and often unnoticed things that I see the sneering face of injustice as it subtly degrades our sexuality right before our eyes. The words of Paul in Philippians 4, that we should keep our minds on things that are noble and pure, seem to have become a nice saying from the past: it's a struggle to maintain it in the present.

Countless times I have listened to heartbreaking stories from friends of mine as they poured out their life stories to me over a cup of tea. I am surrounded by some of the most amazing men and women on the planet whose own parents don't seem to notice them, and have instead taken more pleasure in telling them that they are worthless than in seeing the gold that they helped bring into this world. Many of my friends have suffered abuse and exploitation at the hands of people that they were supposed to have been able to trust and are now left to try to pick up the pieces, being expected to know how to love well even though they've been deprived of it themselves. I have looked into many pairs of beautiful eyes that have given up on hope and instead stare in self-hatred when they look in the mirror, and are more attracted to getting out of life than continuing to live it. These are all injustices that we have become so used to seeing and hearing about that we label them as normal and slip into believing that not much can be done about it.

There have been many occasions when I have stopped myself from letting an angry rant tumble out of my mouth as I have encountered the different faces of injustice, and equally there have been just as many times when I have let myself speak. I want the walk of my life to do the talking though so that words will only add to my actions. I do not want to be a clanging bell or a crashing cymbal that only serves to annoy those within listening distance. I want my voice to be beautiful and my words precious and life-giving to those who hear them.

Justice is a way of life and it beckons us all to step into it. It knows how to love the tender heart of a woman and responds to the need for affirmation that it sees behind heavily painted eyes. It doesn't just give out words but takes the time to sit and simply love until those eyes no longer need to flirt with lust to know that they are beautiful. Justice sets out with eyes and heart wide open and doesn't come home until restoration is complete. It calls forth true identity and sets the captives running free.

3 July 2012

Picture a beautiful sunny morning in New York, clearly the beginnings of a hot day in the sprawling city. It was one of those mornings that makes you want to sing, and even if you have absolutely no vocal talent, makes you believe you sound like an angel. It was glorious and as I walked the few blocks from my apartment to the subway station, I happily thanked God for my life and all that he had blessed me with.

I was doing that half-run, half-skip thing that you do when you're happy, wearing a summer dress and making my way down a flight of stairs, when I entered the subway station. From the base of the stairs to the turnstiles was a mid-sized corridor during the length of which I pulled out my metro card, keeping movement as a continuous flow. As I approached the entrance gates, two guys were walking in front of me and rather than swiping through the turnstiles as is normally required, they walked through the fire exit door that stood open: another unusual occurrence.

Now, I come from the UK, a country where it is quite normal for turnstiles to not be working, therefore requiring alternative entrance points. It's not uncommon to walk through the wrong door but there's usually someone there to point this out to you and steer you in the right direction. You may get a stern look from a security guard but generally there's a belief in a thing called grace and an understanding that there are definitely worse crimes!

Back in 181st St subway station I barely thought twice before following the two guys through the fire exit entrance, metro card still in hand, as I assumed the turnstiles weren't working. I was momentarily puzzled but didn't dwell on it. What's to dwell on when you have a paid fare anyway?

Within thirty seconds of walking through I was in the elevator with a few others, ready to descend to the platform, when a guy stopped the door from closing and asked if I could step outside for a second. I obliged, a little confused, and joined him in the corridor as the elevator doors closed behind me.

'Why didn't you pay for your train fare?'

The question got directed at me in a slightly accusatory fashion and I frowned as my brain tried to figure out what was happening, before answering, 'Oh I have paid, here's my monthly pass.' I pulled out the metro card that I'd just put away to show him. Two cops were watching us from either end of the corridor. I began to twig that these guys were all together but still I didn't sense any real trouble, I mean this was just a simple misunderstanding, right?

The guy looked at me again and repeated the question, asking why I hadn't swiped through. So I sent back my defence, 'I'm sorry I didn't realize that I'd done anything wrong. I have my pass here but can go and swipe through for you now if there's a problem.'

The cops all looked at each other. One of them shrugged at the guy I was stood with, 'It's up to you.' He then reached in his pocket and pulled out a pair of handcuffs. 'Turn around please.'

'Are you serious?!' I looked at him slightly incredulously at the absurdity of what he was about to do.

'Turn around please,' he repeated the command and I found myself obliging, automatically bringing my hands behind my back.

The cold steel clamped around my wrists in a grip that was tighter and more uncomfortable than I'd seen it look on TV. I leant against the cold, tile wall in my summer dress and pearls, handcuffed.

I was definitely not their usual prisoner, the double takes and outright stares from passers-by gave that away, and you could almost hear the questions of 'what did she do?!' as they looked me up and down.

It's a very disabling feeling to be arrested in a foreign country for a crime that has not been specified to you and that you're pretty sure you didn't commit.

My curiosity for what it feels like to wear handcuffs has been well and truly killed! It doesn't feel that great. I tried the whole wriggling manoeuvre to make it more comfortable, again like I'd seen my TV heroes do, but it didn't help. So I remained pinned back, holding my head high to avoid bowing to the inevitable shame that was trying to surround me, and smiling at those who made eye contact with me.

About twenty minutes after being arrested I was stood in the local precinct with two other lucky guys who shared the same fate as me. We were searched, our belongings taken off of us and escorted to a holding cell.

I was sat in there on my own for about an hour, feeling hot tears attempting to choke my throat and swallowing them back down, in a stubborn refusal to let this reduce me to an emotional woman in a dirty cell. There was a toilet opposite that I had had the joy of being searched in, and on the floor was littered someone's hair and bodily fluid: not very welcoming to a new arrival.

It was two hours after my arrest before I was allowed to make that famous call that we all know we have the right to. I couldn't wait to hear Phillip's voice and at the same time didn't know quite how to break the news that I was currently sat in a cell. I had been on my way downtown to meet him and a friend of mine for breakfast, so when I finally spoke to him I was an hour and a half late.

The relief in his voice was unmistakable when my call connected to him and I immediately felt more sure of myself. Phillip knows me, he knows that I'm not a criminal, he'll know that this is all just a big mistake.

No matter how sure of your innocence you may be, sitting in a cell can make you question that fact, even if just for a second.

A further hour and a half after my short conversation with Phillip and I was released back into the New York heat with a ticket to appear in court in July tucked into my bag. It really is such a bizarre feeling to go from being treated like a criminal one minute to being just another tourist in a mass of people the next. It definitely wasn't the introduction to American life that I was aiming for.

So now 'Judgement Day' is just two days away, when a judge gets to decide whether or not they think I'm guilty or innocent for a crime I didn't even know I committed. Welcome to America. Welcome to freedom.

In July 2012 I encountered a new side of what injustice looks like as I fought to maintain my innocence in front of US officials. My case was eventually dismissed in court which thankfully resulted in the whole event being wiped from my record. The time between getting arrested and having my case closed in court was a very vulnerable one for me though, as suddenly I found my character and identity coming under close scrutiny from everyone to whom I spoke. The immediate response or look that I received from anyone in a position of authority in the States was that I was a criminal, and at times I had to really remind myself that I wasn't.

I returned to the UK whilst my court case was being resolved and contacted various people who have known me for long periods, if not my whole life, to get written character references from them. I received the first one from one of my pastors at church and immediately burst into tears as I read it. Her words were so loving and honest, carrying an authority that silenced the voices that I'd been hearing that were telling me I was wrong and deserved the circumstance in which I now found myself. It was then that I realized just how much I needed someone to believe in me and stand up in my defence.

Justice is the one that defends the cause of the weak and speaks on behalf of the voiceless. It hates manipulation and despises webs of lies. Injustice doesn't always look obvious and may often disguise itself behind normality, title or position but it still continues to breed in every area of society. Its aim is to position you in such a way that you begin to forget who you really are and instead put on a cloak of shame and lies that hinders you from moving forward into your true destiny.

As well as being a very unpleasant ordeal to go through, the arrest also massively affected what I had planned for the remainder of the year and meant that the wedding that Phillip and I had begun to organize had to be postponed. It forced us into a long stretch of distance, as I had to return to the UK and he remained in the States, which had the potential to put massive strain on our relationship. There are times when it will feel like the blockages are relentless to seeing your dreams come true but that doesn't mean that the vision is wrong. If it seems slow in coming, wait. The dream is on its way; it will come right on time.

At different times over the last few years my heart has burned for justice as my eyes have been opened further to the levels of injustice in this world. I have learnt more and more to channel that burning towards God in prayer, and to move myself to action when his prompting permits.

31 August 2010

God, where is your justice?!

Lord, hear the cries of your children and let justice flow like a mighty river, righteousness like a never-ending stream!

I feel sick to my stomach, my throat is dry and anger is bubbling beneath my skin. How dare they? How dare he?! How dare Satan enslave, rape, murder God's children? How dare he?!

I found a new hatred for Satan. I hate him. I hate his schemes. I hate him.

Satan's time is up in this land. He is not going to have this nation's purity. He is not going to have this nation's sexuality. He is not going to have this nation's freedom. It is over.

We cannot sit back and wait for someone else to loose the chains. Our eyes have seen, our ears have heard and now our hands must do.

It is time for action, for a fresh mobilization. God, show me, bring your revelation. Teach me your plan, reveal to me your ways. I cannot sit in silence.

I do not want to become a victim of injustice but I want to be a woman who overcomes it, who makes it the platform on which I stand to declare that justice has won the day. I will not be defeated by handcuffs, by a broken heart, by disappointment or loneliness but I set my gaze with determination to see every good thing happen.

It can be easier sometimes to believe that our dreams won't be fulfilled, that the vision won't come to pass or that the injustice around us is too large to overcome, but actually the truth is that good things are on the way, they are just around the corner. If I bow my head to the negative circumstances that I find myself in, or let my past insecurities and brokenness speak the loudest in my life, then I've just allowed injustice to win another hand. I haven't seen all of my dreams fulfilled yet but I know that they are within grasp and I know that if I keep holding on I will see a glorious conclusion.

> *Brothers and sisters, I do not consider myself yet to have taken hold of it. But one thing I do: forgetting what is behind and straining towards what is ahead, I press on towards the goal to win the prize for which God has called me heavenwards in Christ Jesus.*
> *(Philippians 3:13,14)*

Epilogue:

Love

I'm just a normal, everyday woman; there's nothing very extraordinary about me. I get up, go to work; try to keep a tidy home and spend time with friends talking about everything from climate change to that new reality TV show. I get emotional, I laugh and cry, get angry and passionate and hope that my tears over a matter will change something.

The only thing that is truly extraordinary in me and in my story is love. God's love.

When I think about my relationship with God and what it was like when I first encountered him, the best way of describing it is like I had fallen right in front of him, just after messing up. You know when you do something wrong and you fall, those big heavy falls that bruise your knees and knock the breath out of you? That's how I'd fallen, right in front of his feet.

Behind me was this mess, I mean real, broken mess; everyone could see it. But he just looked at me lovingly. And this was when I really fell: I fell in love.

I've fallen in love a few times, fallen in different ways with different people. But this love . . . this love captivates, saturates, envelopes, dethrones and enthrones, covers with no holes, surprises but does not scare, is just simply there.

He just loved me. Not a predatory kind of love, but pure love: a love that doesn't look at me as a woman first, thinking that I am less than or not worthy because of my gender, but as a person; as me. As me with all my stupid thoughts, my selfish decisions, my wayward past; as me with all my hopes and dreams, my desires to overcome and succeed, to be better than my past; as me who just wants to be accepted and loved.

And then I was at his feet again, those same feet that I had fallen in front of before. He held out his hand to me, that same hand that had pulled me out of my broken mess. It felt different this time. It was wounded by the nails that had held it to the cross, but it was healed. It had been into death but here it was alive in my hand. Alive.

Life! The fullness of presence returned, glorious, not broken; full. And the love . . . the love that had led me, the love that I move for has led me back to my knees in awe.

This is the love that can turn a seemingly ordinary life into an extraordinary one. It is this love that I have allowed into my life, letting it lead me all over the world and back again, giving it permission to restore me where I have become broken and renew my hope when I have become disheartened. This is what propels me to keep searching for God's beautiful pearls, those men and women caught in the grasp of injustice, and help to show them that healing is possible, restoration is possible and love is theirs if they want it.

For God so loved the world that he gave his one and only Son,
that whoever believes in him shall not perish but have
eternal life.
(John 3:16)

Contacts

Within this book there are many stories that highlight topics that you may feel passionate about and want to do something about too. It could also be that you need a helping hand to overcome some traumas. Below are the details of several organizations around the world that are working to help the world's most vulnerable people and to see men and women alike live life to their fullest potential.

Pure Creative Arts
20 Springwood Avenue
Liverpool
L19 4TX
UK
Phone: +44 (0)151 427 6777
Email: info@purecreativearts.co.uk
Website: www.purecreativearts.co.uk

STOP THE TRAFFIK International Office
75 Westminster Bridge Road
London SE1 7HS
UK
Phone: +44 (0)207 921 4258

Email: info@stopthetraffik.org
Website: www.stopthetraffik.org

Avalanche Missões Urbanas
Rua Wilson Freitas, 250-Center
Vitória/ES
29016-340
BRAZIL
Phone: +55 (27) 30252452
Email: contato@avalanchemissoes.org
Website: www.avalanchemissoes.org

Dton Naam Ministries, Inc.
PO Box 10649
Midwest City
OK 73140
USA
Email: info@dtonnaam.org
Website: www.dtonnaam.org

NightLight International (Bangkok)
PO Box 1414
Nana Post Office
Bangkok
THAILAND
10112
Email: bkk@nightlightinternational.com
Website: nightlightinternational.com

Golddigger Trust
PO Box 4246
Sheffield
S17 9AW
UK
Email: info@golddiggertrust.co.uk
Website: www.golddiggertrust.co.uk

Global Children's Movement
PO Box 9204
Glendale
CA 91226
USA
Email: admin@gcmovement.org
Website: www.gcmovement.org

Streetwise Project
PO Box 38
Wavertree
Liverpool
L15 0FH
UK
Phone: +44 (0)151 733 3373
Email: admin@streetwiseproject.com
Website: www.streetwiseproject.com

Notes

1   UN definition of human trafficking www.unode.org.
2   Statistics provided by www.unglobalcompact.org.